Wakefield Press

Sex, Knives & Bouillabaisse

Teri Louise Kelly lives in Adelaide, South Australia, with her partner Mel Kelly, where together they find yet more ways to defy convention.

Sex, Knives & Bouillabaisse

Teri Louise Kelly

Wakefield Press

Wakefield Press
1 The Parade West
Kent Town
South Australia 5067
www.wakefieldpress.com.au

First published 2008

Cover designed by Liz Nicholson, designBITE
Text designed and typeset by Clinton Ellicott, Wakefield Press
Printed and bound by Hyde Park Press, Adelaide

National Library of Australia
Cataloguing-in-publication entry

Author:	Kelly, Teri Louise.
Title:	Sex, knives & bouillabaisse/author, Teri Louise Kelly.
Publisher:	Kent Town, S. Aust.: Wakefield Press, 2008.
ISBN:	978 1 86254 756 8 (pbk.).
Subjects:	Kelly, Teri Louise.
	Cooks – Australia – Biography.
	Women cooks – Australia – Biography.
	England – Biography.
Dewey Number:	641.5092

Publication of this book was assisted by the Commonwealth Government through the Australia Council, its arts funding and advisory body.

TO MEL, MY OWN JO BUCK,

THANKS FOR THE TUITION,

IN EVERYTHING.

This Bouillabaisse a noble dish is –
A sort of soup or broth, or brew,
Or hotchpotch, of all sorts of fishes,
That Greenwich never could outdo;
Green herbs, red peppers, mussels, saffern,
Soles, onions, garlic, roach, and dace;
All these you eat at Terre's tavern,
In that one dish of Bouillabaisse.

From *The Ballad of Bouillabaisse*
W.M. Thackeray

Contents

A SHORT GLOSSARY OF USEFUL KITCHEN TERMINOLOGY FOR THE UNINITIATED

Aboyer – Brute with booming voice who calls dockets to section grunts during service.

Aromates – All herbs, roots and pig-bin scraps with a tasty flavour and bouquet still pleasant to the nose.

Arsehole – Any member of the kitchen brigade stupid enough to not follow a directive from a superior brigade member to the letter.

Bastarde – Term of endearment used by foreign waiters to chefs upon receipt of the staff meal.

Black hole – The place where your uniforms always vanish.

Boner – A knife used in butchery or an unexpected erection. (Best to check before accepting compliment.)

Book (The) – *Le Répertoire de La Cuisine*, the apprentice chef's midnight reading.

Chambermaid – Any loosely principled girl.

Clog – Preferred choice of footwear in the asylum.

Commis – A young person recently grabbed off the street by F&B men attired solely in black.

Dak – The procedure of pulling down another chef's pants so that anyone passing can admire the view.

Despot – The Chef de Cuisine.

Duce – As above, or: The Big Cheese, The Man, Boss Hogg, Mein Fuehrer.

Dumb waiter – Self-explanatory.

F&B/S.O.B. – Food & Beverage. Term used to describe any person who wears a suit and tie.

Farce – A service performed by unqualified personnel – such as breakfast chefs.

Front of house – A place where anyone who feels they are better than any other staff member sits around all day doing nothing.

Gimp/Geek/Goon/Grunt – Shitheads like me.

Gratiner – To pass something otherwise rancid under a salamander once it has been lavishly slathered with shredded cheese-board leftovers.

Hatch – A small hole in a wall et cetera where beer is served.

Larder – A place in the kitchen where those who cannot stomach front-line combat huddle in groups behind butcher's blocks.

Lurgy – Any kind of communicable disease spread amongst hotel staff.

Maul – Usually started over something trivial such as ownership of a knife, woman, beer, chef's jacket.

Merde – Kitchen slang for 'Oh bother'.

Mise-en-place (meez) – The shit you need to prep the menu.

Noddy – Any apprentice or brigade member who continually nods while being instructed.

Paner – To egg and breadcrumb any food product so that paying customer/staff member will not realize that said food-stuff has turned green.

Plat à sauter – Shallow bottom fry pan, usually of copper, that can be reddened over intense heat and then plopped straight into the nearest dishwasher's bare hands.

Pilaff – Fancy sounding name for a rice dish made from leftover ingredients.

Réduire – To reduce any sauce or stock by vigorous boiling until the pan has to be thrown out.

Sauté – To cook rapidly – the 'get out of the shit' manoeuvre.

Slops – Staff food.

Sous Chef (sous) – Egg-sucking dog, second-in-command, a man with one eye on the top job and the other on casual 'skirt'.

Somage – The worst word heard in a kitchen – yelled out before the grand announcement of yet another late diner's eight-course fucking meal.

'You won't be surprised that diseases are innumerable – count the cooks.'

SENECA

'Heaven sends us good meat, but the Devil sends cooks.'

DAVID GARRICK

'There's no money in professional football kid, why not get yourself a real job instead? Like that cooking gig, people always have to eat you know.'

MY FATHER

SUBZERO

This installment of my lurid memoirs will, I think, enlighten you on many points related both to professional cookery and other more vexed issues. You will laugh, I trust, and maybe, if you are the kind of reader who associates by default, you might even feel for me now and again. All of that is as it should be in the incestuous relationship that is author and reader; I could ask no more, but undoubtedly, I will.

You might, as you near the rump end of this memoir, begin to experience confusion over certain of my allusions. I wouldn't blame you, and as I am by nature a warm-hearted and sympathetic kind of girl I am going to mitigate any issues that might play on your mind in the future: this memoir not only blankets some of my time spent on the ranges but also a lot of the time I lived and was known as cute and cheeky little Luiz, *the boy*.

So, by now you've re-read the cover and if you're half as clever as you look you'll have pretty much sussed what's occurring, right? Good-O. And for those of you who obviously aren't that bright, let me shed some extra wattage on the scene. While I was born Luiz the boy, I took it upon myself to defy nature, God, family and society, and did what hadn't been done properly the first time: that is, I amended my gender.

There, you see, how hard was that? So Luiz is me, albeit a

me that has since been expunged by the healing hands and wonder drugs of modern medicine. Nowadays I am Teri Louise. This of course is neither the time nor place to venture deeply into that part of my peculiar life; there will be time enough as you and I come to know one another more intimately. For now all you need do is fulfil the Devil's bargain you have struck with me by buying this book. I am as certain as I can be, given that I am pumped full of more hormones than a battery chicken, that despite what I've just told you in the strictest confidence – you won't hold it against me. We are, after all, adults. All good upstanding citizens of whatever coalition is going around.

Therefore without further fanfare I hereby permit you to begin turning pages, you pays your money and you takes your chances, okay? Enjoy!

ZERO

The events I am going to recall for you herewith, took place in Brighton in the south east of England in the late 1970s or thereabouts – apart from the bit in Paris, which occurred in France. And the piece set in the West Country of England, which occurred in . . . well, hotshit, you'll work it out, you look smart enough.

It all started in 1975. I was fifteen years, three hundred and forty-four days old, nothing but a kid, albeit a kid they'd highlighted in *The Year Book* as a 'hard case'. I was four months out of juvey, give or take, and I had a swagger, an edge, abrasion. I rubbed people up the wrong way and if those who'd been thus rubbed wanted 'some', back then I was always ready to oblige.

Talk is cheap however, it always has been, and believe you me, action always talks louder than words. That's the way of life, in the schoolyard, in the showers before lights out, and in the big white world of professional cookery.

I'll be fine, Mum, I told her as she sobbed. If you don't get no mail you know I'm in jail! But that only made her sob harder. Mothers, eh?

I'd been chosen, again. For what reason I didn't know, but whatever, I was going to be still-birthed again without the use of forceps. We went to the big hotel on a Sunday, if I recall, and on the Saturday I'd had my head shaved again. No punk was going to think I was some tightly wound-up fresh-faced kid without a clue. The first shithead who called my bluff would be regretting it for one hell of a while – yeah, I was ready, I'd been called and when I'm called, friends, you can always bank on me rocking up ready to rumble . . .

So, like the saying goes, many are chosen but few are called, and I can't quite recall who said that, or even if it's wholly accurate but who fucking cares, right? But maybe those immortal words, or words just like them, were first spoken by that giant of professional cookery Auguste Escoffier.

Gus, as the boys knew him, ruled his ranges with an iron will and a fierce determination to see professional cookery flourish not only as a venerable career, but also a recognized form of the more sophisticated of the arts. And art it has become, I suppose, although whether Gus or Carême or Brillat-Savarin would recognize it as such if they fell forward through time and landed in a trendy bistro-cum-café-cum-wine-bar with a chef wearing hot-pink pants, a Metallica T-shirt and two Pirates of the Caribbean earrings, lord only knows.

Still, this is progress I suspect, and many of those dedicated professionals I once waged war with warned me to take careful heed of that very thing, progress, just before they left our ilk for good on the happy bus. I was young then, young and irresponsible with a huffy bravado that is the backbone of all the young fools gullible enough to stumble into professional cookery as a job.

Although honestly, the only resemblance that cookery has to other 'jobs' is that you do get paid for doing it – eventually, after long and spirit-breaking court cases. Gus never worried too much about money, I guess, he was happy with his ranges and his pig's trotters, with his grives et merles and canard guts, Gus was a simple man. Thereafter followed a whole string of simple men, hung up like beef sausages in a butcher's window, men with a loose foothold in the land of integrity and a heavy dependency on girlish good looks and very unsophisticated charm, renegades one and all from the civilized world. Cookery would take away from them their finest years and, in most if not all cases, leave them burned out and in rehab at an age when in other jobs they would be reaching a mid-life peak of stability with kids and a mortgage to fret about. For by the time most chefs sober up around their mid thirties, life has all but passed them by; and by then they are too physically wrecked for any other kind of job and too mentally decrepit to be seriously considered for anything other than long-term unemployment or breaking and entering.

Not me though. I managed to circumvent the globe, avoid multiple bogus charges for income tax evasion and quit The Game with enough of my liver intact to still live a life outside of those overbearing windowless walls. Okay, so my podiatrist says that I'll never get rid of that gnarled skin on my feet, and those calluses will stay with me for life – but hey, that's a small price to pay considering I still have use of most of the faculties I blindly entered that world with. Sure, I fled the scene of my many crimes at a relatively old age for a career chef, and I still sometimes find myself hankering for those bygone days – mulling over events and reminiscing about all the very weird characters who frequent hotel kitchens and indeed hotels. It is, as they say, a surreal kind of secular life, one lived not by clocks and bus timetables or Saturday shopping, but by some instinctive ritual that stirs you at three in the morning when you only climbed into a bed, even if it ain't your own, at one forty-five.

On many levels, it's nothing but institutionalization, for living-in, in large hotels, is just like being detained in Borstal. Your chef de cuisine is little more than the headmaster or warden and the walls are always the same soul-destroying colour – and you, you're just a worthless hunk of flesh waiting to be dry humped by the whole brigade. Your arse is grass.

So, I'm gonna tell you about it, like it was you know? I'm ready to squeal, fully prepared to point the finger, and ready to swear on a stack of *Le Répertoire de La Cuisine* (hereafter referred to as The Book) that what I'm going to tell you in this rather sordid book is as close to the truth as you're ever likely to get. And the truth, as maybe you're aware, is sometimes the most unpalatable thing of all to keep down . . . far worse than fresh-shucked oysters on a shitter of a new dawn. So bottoms up. They say that a lot, in professional kitchens – most usually after service when there's just you and two long-armed spooks with the need for speed on their minds.

Anyhow, any probs you can contact me collect at –

C/-
Poste Restante
Main PO
La Paz
Bolivia

1.

All Together For The Floral Dance

Nineteen seventy-five was a good year to be young, better than say 1935, although the music was average: Rod Stewart and his Maggie May were prolonging the use of tartan as a fashion accessory, some old dinosaurs were bellowing about a whiter shade of pale, Abba was consistently hitting all of the right three notes and leading the push for full satin daywear, and Elton John still sported what remained of his own hair. Kids were wearing large platform heels and dangerously wide flared pants, the afro was in and so was Newcastle Brown Ale. Georgie Best, the fifth Beatle footballer, had fled to Spain (again), Terry Wogan – he of the fucking Floral dance – was the hip DJ, and no dimwit of a prime minister could get a grip on either inflation or football hooliganism.

On the personal front, my hopes of a career in professional football had been seriously dashed by the West Sussex constabulary, my old man and Queen Elizabeth II.

At school, in the concrete zoo, I had been mistakenly fingered for arson and after that, they didn't hold out much in the way of hope for a scallion like me. Still, to give them due credit, they persevered, even to the extent of doctoring up some good pupil reports for me to take along to the interview they'd arranged at the big hotel. Sure, I told the interviewers confidently, I'm a fucking gourmand with a frying pan. That must have clinched it because no sooner was I back pasting up pictures of Catwoman in my bedroom than the old fella came bursting in swinging a new suitcase like he'd just won a free trip on the Orient Express. I was off, apparently – off me bloody head. I had a brand new suitcase, a roll of exceedingly dangerous-looking knives and some clownish pants that looked like pyjama bottoms. Your old fella always knows best ... doesn't he?

Sure, but I wasn't thinking that on the drive to my new home away from home. In fact, I wasn't thinking about anything much; I was used to long drives with a blanket over me head, but let me tell you since that day I've never accepted rides from strangers, or family members.

Don't sweat it, kid, my old man said casually while he flicked another cheroot out the car window and it came hurtling back into my lap like Halley's fucking comet. As I brushed off the sparks I thought, you know, Luiz, you're better off in some big hotel, at least there you'll be burn proof. I always have been you know? Touch wood.

Being a chef is a pretty neat job, it's wild, a hellfire ride on the back of a screaming hog, the kind of career choice the reckless make ... yeah, the young and the reckless, that's us.

So how do you score a job like this? you ask breathlessly. A job where you can swagger around like the despot in some small African country? Well, it's not easy, friends, not easy at all. What you need is a slice of luck, troubled adolescent years and a careers advisor too dumb to appreciate just what an opportunity he's giving you because all he sees in front of him is a juvenile delinquent with a checkered school report card and a leery smirk. Shit! It's exactly this kind of CV that makes most hotel food and beverage managers grin that malicious grin that they live to grin, for what better candidate could you hope for as an apprentice chef in a big hotel kitchen?

Before you know it you're en route to a live-in life with a whole swag of lethal weaponry and heavily starched uniforms stashed in the new suitcase your old man got you as a leaving-home gift.

Your mum's already turning your bedroom into a sewing nook and your old man is counting up how much he'll save a week in bog roll alone. They've got you out of the nest quicker than they could ever have hoped for and all without the need for legal paperwork. They turn you out on to the street right in front of the big imposing doors and the billowing canopy and you stand there craning your neck to see daylight as the elegantly top-hatted and tailed doorman comes down thinking you're a tipping guest; and to be sure, he's nice enough to your folks, who go home muttering about how great it all is – what a big adventure! And then before your old man's even braked to go around the corner the doorman is calling you a filthy little butt wipe and warning you never to appear in his line of sight again.

I didn't know squat about cookery, and even less about the inner workings of big hotels – I didn't know for example that hotel kitchens, and even big imposing hotels, aren't for the faint of heart, or anyone who has been diagnosed as clinically sane. That in fact they're dank cavernous environments that smell of rotting food, decomposing brain matter, bad personal hygiene and stale beer.

That they're a world, nay a universe, away from the grandeur of the elegant dining room with its silky smooth waiters and doyen diners far above, and indeed, another universe away from the life you knew only fifteen minutes ago, because way down in the subterranean heat and humidity of the industrial kitchen the normal laws of the civilized world cease to exist, just like in Kampala during Daddy's reign of terror.

When you become an apprentice chef in a big hotel kitchen with a brigade forty strong and you're right at the very bottom, you have, inadvertently or otherwise, forfeited rights of ownership over your own life. From that terrible day on, your life is owned and ruled over by the chef de cuisine – a skulking brute of a man with a slurred accent that you can't decipher and a serious binge-drinking problem. In the real world this guy would be in a sanatorium or on some mandatory AA program, but in the surreal world of the hotel kitchen, it is this guy who rules your world with an iron fist and a devious temperament.

I didn't know any of that – right then, I was too busy craning my neck so I could peer heavenwards to see when this mammoth building stopped. The doorman growled at me again. I subdued the urge to stick one on this waster; there was time enough to let these fools know that I was an incendiary device looking for a place to explode. Okay, Jeeves, keep your hat on.

Jeeves goes back inside and some guy who looks disturbingly like Heinrich Himmler comes out and leads me down an alley around prostrate winos where even the rats have more spunk and better food than I'll enjoy for some considerable time. I climb up the fire escape feeling like a refugee from civility and am shown brusquely into a room about the size of my parents' airing cupboard, where, before I can ask why there's other people's stuff in it, the door bangs shut. They've got me now, under lock and key and on a ball and chain. It all starts here and of course I'm bloody starving . . . and I just lie there waiting, wondering who the hell will walk through the door . . .

2.

All The Young Dudes

And then I find out.

I couldn't fail to notice the wide-lapelled white suit laid out on my new roommate's bed. Ye gods, I recall thinking, this is some bad fucking karma. Billy had already earned his kitchen nickname as he'd started work three weeks before me due to the strange quirks of the English school system. Coupled with the fact that Billy was almost a year older than me, this ought to have afforded him an unassailable advantage, but alas poor Billy was a lad with many traits that riled his peers in the great white desert, like his accent.

The first time I saw him, when he came into what was now our room, I thought someone had made a terrible mistake. He must have too, especially as I was casually playing with a flick knife. No way could this guy be a first-year apprentice – he looked like my granddad.

Ay up, he said to me, in his rich Midlands brogue, I'm Billy. He had a handshake like a vicar, and after he'd lit a smoke I sat there listening to him rabbit on – and holding his fag like a woman – no way would me and this guy ever hit it off.

Yes indeed, Billy Shivers, so christened due to his tendency to exhibit nervousness by way of trembling uncontrollably, always struck me as an odd candidate for an environment like a professional kitchen. Billy was a forty-five-year-old guy inside a seventeen-year-old's body who doted on the Stylistics, those jive funking soul brothers who be-bopped in choreographed unison with Colgate smiles. Billy was a disco pig, a grooving fourth Bee Gee with male-pattern balding already well established and a pickup routine that might have worked well in an M6 truck stop, but didn't have a hope in hell down south where the girls are more savvy.

Cracking birds, man! he told me excitedly. I already knew that if Billy got laid it would be flat out on an emergency-ward stretcher.

Billy's main disadvantage, you see, was that he hailed from some Midlands place where a pickled onion with your fish and chips was still considered a big night out. That dour northern tenacity and dry humour didn't serve him well in the midst of so many wide boys on the make for a quid. When Billy cracked a joke – and I have to admit that Billy's sardonic dryness grew on you like bitch tits when you got to really know him – nobody laughed, and the more no one laughed the more Billy withdrew into his shell. Of all the attributes new apprentices require to stay the course, fortitude is amongst the highest ranking, a huge serve of indomitable spirit, a belief in one's own resources and ability. Like I said, Billy's one-month head start ought to have given him an advantage over me, only it hadn't.

Billy had struggled morosely through his own pot-wash stint with clinical depression and a furrowed brow. Little John and his filthy gang of dilettantes had sapped what spirit Billy possessed with their constant mimicking of his accent and his nervous disposition, and he had been in the main kitchen just one day when I first met him. Fortunately for me, and vice versa for Billy I suppose, he was able to fill me in on the main headcases to avoid and so I ventured into that heinous world armed with at least some little knowledge of procedure and characters, and for that leg-up I was eternally grateful to Billy.

Who you follow? he asked me.

Man United, I replied.

Ah, shite – we ain't gonna get along! I hate Man United!

Despite that, we would, as all alien room buddies must, forge an alliance that would never have occurred in the big world outside. Where Billy was reticent, I was fiery, Billy remained angrily silent and I let it fly verbally – in these ways we somehow complemented each other and over time we'd become friends as well as allies. And we'd need to, for within eighteen hard months, due to circumstances far beyond our control, and fraud like you could never imagine, the hotel we had grown comfortably into like a pair of well-loved slippers would be jettisoned by the chain that then owned it. Liquidating of assets I believe they call it on the markets. A move that would effectively catapult Billy and me into a whole new hostile environment, where again we would find ourselves back at the bottom of a very spiteful pecking order. Yes indeed, those were bad and ugly days but that is for later. Right now we shall meet the brigade of the hotel me and Billy first started off in, a big rambling place full of corridors and people with double-barrelled job titles, a place where everyone had a certain pride in their work and where two superstar apprentices made their albeit dirty marks.

The boys above us, Will and Ben, as we shall know them from hereon in, were peas in the pod. They were school friends who had somehow wangled a gig as apprentices at the same goddamned hotel – inseparable street urchins with a penchant for Levis, Brut 33, Rod Stewart, that 'orrible North London football outfit known as Tottenham fucking Hotspur, and any Homo Sapien who happened to have a useable orifice. Will and Ben didn't share a room like the rest of us; they cohabited in a boudoir, a veritable knocking shop where somehow the fiends in question had bribed the night porters not only to furnish them with an endless supply of knocked-off mini-bar drinks, but also to escorting said orificed homo sapiens to and from said boudoir. All night long me and Billy would lay in our hovel listening to the likely lads going at it like lifers on conjugal visits, listening to giggling girls, heavy panting, and Maggie fucking May a hundred times a night as their headboard continually thumped against our wall emitting the same repetitious rhythm you hear in the crowd when Brazil are playing football. You learn fast; there is no such thing as privacy when you're bunked up 24/7 with shower buddies.

It was inevitable, I guess, that a war would break out. There are many incidents that are jolly pranks and indeed can be taken in the spirit of such, and there are events that are far more insidious. No matter what people say, there is no fine line between pleasure and pain, the two are as far apart as lobster and potted shrimps. No sooner had we settled in, than strange and unnatural events began to occur – first it would be our room looking like it had been raided by the drugs squad after we returned from shift, then fish guts started turning up in our beds – or urine stains, or a used tampon. And seeing as how the Überfräulein who oversaw the laundry was hot on the 'one set of sheets per week' rule, once your bedding was fouled you had to wait another squalid week for replacements. On and on this misery dragged until finally I at least could take no more, and, egged on by me, me and Billy undertook a lightning raid next door while Will and Ben got feather cuts someplace. Man, what a trashing we gave that room, and after we'd finished we unloaded the Brut 33 so the whole room looked like some surreal Christmas gig thrown by Rod the Mod himself. After that, we barricaded our own door and hung tight for the fallout. And fall out it did, for no sooner had the boys returned to find their inner sanctuary violated than they began trying to hack through our door with a cleaver they'd borrowed from the cold larder. Christ Almighty, it was like *The Shining*, the sound of cheap plywood splintering and the door latch busting out of its bracket – we were in for it.

The door caved in, and Will and Ben right along with it. They could see their quarry and it was about then we let the fire extinguisher off, yeah, it had been my idea as some kind of fallback plan and I'd given no thought to the consequences. Here we were, not even three months on the job, going hand-to-hand on the fifth floor of a swanky hotel with two of our peers. Retaliation came, of course, as we four now squared off cheek to jowl in the debris of what was once a quite livable room – two cockney wide boys with ruined hair and two kids with spots and bad hair. I can't remember who swung first, but I do recall I got off one of those lucky haymakers. By the intervention of Jesus himself it didn't catch Will, but instead made him swing his noggin back so violently that he nutted his offsider in the eye; and the resulting shiner Ben sported for a fortnight thereafter was a joy to behold.

After that it was all rough and tumble and handbags at five paces, but the damage had been done. Ten minutes later we were too knackered to carry on and all four of us sat there licking our wounds and laughing like kids after a schoolyard stoush – until it dawned on Will and Ben just how much we'd wrecked two rooms and most of a corridor.

Now those boys had trod a wavering line between kitchen immortality and adolescent delinquency – they had already received both verbal and written warnings from management for their antics, like tossing a full ice bucket out of their window that had gone straight through the hotel's entrance canopy and almost decapitated some OAP about to venture out for an after-dinner constitutional. They had been the instigators of the great shaving-foam fight that had covered an entire landing with the stuff, and been accused of stealing the wheels from the sommelier's car mid service hoicking the old Austin up on breeze blocks. A gig like this one could have ended their tenure there and then – all we had to do was squeal like two piglets at a gold record smorgasbord for Benny and Bjorn.

But instead, as you'd expect, we spent the remainder of the night cleaning up like some mad skit from *The Benny Hill Show* until the two rooms looked about as respectable as they were ever going to be – until all we had to contend with was the door, or what was left of it. How in the hell were we going to explain that one? Easy, the lads told us, just say that you went for a walk and when you came back it was like that! We'll back you up. Ye gods, I have done some hare-brained things, but going down to management to report that my bedroom door had been all but turned to kindling while I was out taking some air really took some beating. F&B ran the rule over me, telling me the police would have to be called and that most likely Billy and me would have to share the cost of a replacement door via deductions from our already featherweight wage packets . . . The lads said not to sweat it, just like a deckhand on *Titanic* telling steerage passengers not to panic because there were enough lifeboats for all.

Then there were Pig Pen and Bob. Pig Pen hadn't earned his name because he ponged; he had won it through his addiction to those *Peanuts* books that were all the rage when we first started our own lives of slavery. Pig Pen was a hippy, a flower child with a long ponytail and a pacifist demeanour just made for the pastry section, and it was there among the marzipan and the food colourings that he had made his home.

But Bob was a nut job. He had finished his apprenticeship and there wasn't one person in the whole brigade who was sorry about that. Bob had finally qualified and the apprentices, especially, breathed a collective sigh of relief because Bob had this special party trick, and not a run of the mill one either. Bob was a biter and a vicious bastard with it. There you were on the line sweating like you've never sweated before, not even when the Transport Police had again nabbed you for fare dodging, when suddenly you had this searing pain in your bum and whatever was in your hands unexpectedly obeyed the laws of gravity.

Everyone on the line, all the apprentices, had the indelible bite mark on their bum, not a love-tap either, no sir, the real bona fide clamp-down, love-at-first bite. The pain was excruciating, but the humiliation was worse. Needless to say when Bob finally found himself a real job the whole kitchen had a party where everyone compared bite marks and reminisced in the way chefs do – with copious amounts of cheap cooking brandy – about just how much fun Bob had been. Yeah, it was a real gas when he grabbed hold of your nipple and tied a cow hitch with it, or maybe caught you unawares in the cold larder and gave you a Chinese burn right on your thigh – Christ, how much more fun could a person want?

After us six there were the section chefs, a constantly fluctuating personnel who read *Soldier Of Fortune* magazine as eagerly as they perused the cookery jobs pages – of which there are hundreds. Some were okay guys with a dedication to duty who set the example to be followed, but others were misfits from society, a hotchpotch of lifers and part-timers devoid of scruples or any kind of principle recognizable on Civvie Street. These guys are the marrow in the bones, a kind of eternally shifting mix of sorry-faced psychopaths each with his own hang-up.

Mick, our first saucier, looked like any of those baddies in a spaghetti western. He had a drop-down handlebar moustache that he was forever trimming while he stirred the day's potage, and a mean, snarling, dog-with-mange temper that could slip its leash over the most innocuous of incidents. Mick was the first and last bastard to kick me in the gooleys during my apprenticeship. Some time after that unsavoury incident the Vice boys turned up and dragged his sorry arse away on charges of illegal earnings from pimping: his own wife, too – I bet that waster is still serving up porridge with hair trimmings in it at some government facility for the retarded.

There was a real old-timer of a pastry chef called Ronnie, who had an identical twin brother called Reggie who worked in the pastry of our sister hotel a couple of blocks away. The Krays they were known as, identical they were, and believe me you had to see them side by side to realize how identical – but in their moods they differed greatly.

Ronnie was a compassionate teacher with a keen sense of humour, whereas Reggie was a sour-faced old bastard who would far have preferred to see apprentices regularly flogged as a part of their training. The Krays had married identical twin sisters and when you got to see all four at a function your mind just boggled. Though the twins sometimes took each other's places in their respective kitchens, after a while we got to know our twin just by his manner of speech. Ronnie never swore at all, he would use 'blooming' as the height of blasphemy, but

Reggie had a mouth like a sewage outlet; every other word was a 'fuck' or 'shit'.

At the top were the two Alans, which was always confusing, although one you called 'Alan' and the other you simply addressed as 'Chef'. Alan, the sous chef, was a white version of Shaft. He had this long Afghan coat and the seventies porn-star moustache, the mirror sunglasses and both a wife and a mistress, which was all very bohemian. The apprentices liked Alan, not only because he threw parties that lasted three days but also because he was a diligent teacher and heavy handed with the booze. Sometimes me and Billy would get to go to one of his infamous love-ins, taken blindfolded in a Mini with twelve people crammed inside to some back street semi-detached pad that had tiger skins on the wall and beads in every doorway. The place always smelt like Afghanistan in summer and was obviously where the beautiful people from the sixties were still clinging to the love and peace ethic. Alan had this laidback kind of gig going where nothing really mattered, man – until, that is, his wife finally had a gutful and threw him and his treasured Jimi Hendrix and Bob Dylan albums onto the street one frosty morning. After that Alan kind of straightened up and there weren't any more parties.

The head chef, the Duce (the other Alan) was a traditionalist who expected the apprentices on his ship to scrub up to his expectations. He was not a brute of a man, but imposing enough with his three-foot-high toque to give us youngsters the impression that he was God himself. I guess this guy must have seen something in me after I came up to the main kitchen from my time in the pot wash, because I spent the next three turgid months plagued with nosebleeds. There I'd be diligently practising my knife skills or listening while a section chef instructed me in stocks and sauces, when for no reason whatsoever my nose would start bleeding. Okay, not for 'no reason'. The reason was that a few years earlier I'd got embroiled in fisticuffs at my supermarket shelf-stacking job, and the kid I got embroiled with had fists like a couple of frozen turkeys. He didn't break my nose, but he must have severely damaged my 'vessels' because since that day any upset or stress just kinda brought on the bleeds. I would have to go sit in the chef's office with my head tilted back and my nose pinched until the damned gushing stopped – which sometimes took up to an hour.

Never once did the Duce get irate about this – he just reckoned it would go away of its own accord, and if it didn't then I'd need to see somebody. Eventually it did stop, and we were all thankful for that because everyone was sick of having to throw out sauces or prep because I'd bled into them. Except for Mick, who just used to stir in another handful of tomato puree to disguise the blood.

So this was the happy team that surrounded Billy and me like an extended family and once our troubles with roommates and nosebleeds had subsided we settled into our new life with its constant clarion calls to arms and ebbs and flows. People came and people went, but the tide always seemed to swirl around me, and I for one believed that this would never change. What a fool I was.

3.

A Whiter Shade Of Pale

I didn't have any worries, apart from malnutrition.

I was the proverbial new kid on the block, and if nature had sweat rashes, the fevers, syphilis, alcohol poisoning and dead skin in store for me, well, that would all come in due course. What I had to deal with first was purgatory – Tom Brown had it fucking easy at private school compared with an apprentice chef in a big swanky hotel, if you ask me. If all you had to fret about was being roasted over an open fire then life would be pretty damned cushy. But you have to worry about more than that, and then more besides.

Food, by way of example. Known only to the devil-may-care hierarchy of big kitchens is some fiendish plot to starve new apprentices into subjugation during the savage indoctrination period known as The Gauntlet. So hungry do new internees become, so gaunt, that many supplement their paltry incomes by moonlighting as supermodels. To many, even a half-chewed piece of avocado covered in some old lady's fuchsia lipstick becomes a prized morsel. If you had money you could of course easily circumvent this sadistic ritual – *if* is the key word however, because somewhere between the interview, that nasty ritual you undertook sitting next to your old man and opposite some Hercule Poirot look-alike, and actually arriving at boot camp, both you and your old man (conveniently) have forgotten that Poirot had expressly told you that new apprentices don't get paid until the end of the first month. So for a month you travel only between the staff elevator and your bed, whether there's anyone else in it or not. Between bed stops you're serving as the butt of many jokes or doing heinously mundane chores such as scrubbing wooden pallets with a well-loved Brillo pad. You're sleeping more, both to stave off malnutrition and to keep up your rapidly diminishing energy levels. Starting work again at five every afternoon is a totally alien concept as you've spent your entire existence to date watching *Blue Peter* at five weekdays while your mum whips up bangers and mash.

Fuck *Blue Peter*, the chefs tell you, *Magpie* was way freaking better anyhow.

What about that Jenny bird huh? they'll say, holding two honeydew melons to their chest for practical illumination purposes. You wanna suck on these bitch, huh?

Don't worry about money kid, your old man had said, you'll be eating lobster every day and getting your room and board – kid, you've fallen on easy street and let me tell you I'm sick with jealousy. Uh huh, your old man fell for it lock and stock after Hercule had told him there had been three hundred applicants for the job you subsequently got – only being a Frenchy, he'd cunningly omitted the part about two hundred and ninety of them still having time to serve in juvenile detention.

Funnily enough, you get used to not eating – even though you're surrounded by enough fine nosh to stock the *QE2* to New York and back. Because it doesn't pass your lips and your sense of smell quits trying to entice your fingers to go to your mouth, pretty soon you're running on nervous energy and facial twitches. Have the balls to grab a stray chip or stick your dirty little fingers into a pot of mashed spud, and some ex-Belsen prison guard will rap you over the knuckles with his palette knife. You can eat staff food, of course, even though it's the worst kind of muck to be found – there's better food in the skip. Make the mistake of showing up half an hour early for your shift in the hope of eating, and some jackal on the prep table will summon you over to dice blanched tomatoes or shred lettuce. You can stand there all you like wistfully staring at the left-over breakfast sausages, but it'll do you no good. Next, the older apprentices start to drift in and fry sirloins that they cover with sauce and garnish with huge home-made chips and half a cauliflower. Those boys know how to eat because they've earned the right, and they laugh right in your face as they saunter past overloaded with French stick, and you just stand there robotically chopping your tomatoes hoping a piece will fall onto your clog rather than the floor so you can shovel it up and enjoy it later in secrecy.

Mercifully, unless you're a complete moron, you don't wear this routine for long, you have to sink or swim, fall back on the wherewithal and guile that had not so long ago landed you in one of Her Majesty's juvenile detention camps for willful destruction of public property and assault on a WPC while she was in the pursuit of her lawful business – the lawful business of trying to apprehend you for willful destruction of public property, to be exact.

Once you appreciate that stealing and cheating aren't frowned upon in large kitchens – that in fact they're traits to be admired and even nurtured – you can let that deviant streak in you bob to the surface like scum on a consommé and you'll soon find ways not only to get at food but also to stop being attacked while you're getting at it. The best way is to have a weapon at hand; a piece of rubber hose or a meat mallet. Better still, even keep a few meathooks in your wrap. There's plenty of vicious-looking equipment lying around a big kitchen and if that half-bent Belgium larder chef thinks he's going to bully you and maybe get into your pants in the bargain, well, let's see how he feels about a whupping with a length of hose.

You want a piece of this action, Brussels, eh?

Sure you don't actually have to do it, well only in the most extreme of cases, but the innuendo lets those around you know that you're the kind of kid with nothing to lose and plenty to gain.

4.

Captain Fantastic And The Brown Dirt Cowboys

It's a dog-eat-dog world, a savage and backbiting existence that begins the very first day you walk into the kitchen attired in whites so bright and clean you look like a blizzard, a hat resting on the bridge of your nose and an apron Mrs Bridges from *Upstairs Downstairs* would be proud of because it's touching your feet. Under your arm is a brand new, as yet unused, set of chefs knives that your folks got engraved with your name to stop them being flogged in week one, and around your neck is a badly tied necktie that's already strangling you. You needn't worry, however, those knives won't see active service for a month or two at least, and you'll learn to tie your necktie properly simply to stop other chefs strangling you with it. You stand there listening to the caterwaul of cat calls and then some rum-addled deadbeat of a chef comes up to you and marches you straight down to the pot wash – and that's where you'll stay for a month at least, knee-deep in slops and elbow deep in scummy brown water.

You start your professional career under the eagle eyes of the winos and derelicts who rule the pot wash with a ball of steel wool in one hand and the smell of beer on their breath. People like Little John, who was the tallest human I had ever seen. Little John was so tall that you couldn't even hear what he was saying to you because your ears weren't attuned to high altitude conversations. If Little John got mad, which he did about six times a day, he would pick up the closest living beast and embrace it in an oxygen-depriving bear hug.

Sometimes if he was just feeling playful he'd dunk some poor bastard into the dish-wash sink just for kicks.

Little John kept half a roll-up behind one ear and a steel comb behind the other. He had been a dapper 'Ted' once, but that kind of gig got too expensive, so instead of fighting Mods on the beach every bank holiday weekend Little John decided to live there instead. Sure it all made sense to me because I agreed with every damned word Little John said. If he said the sky was purple and that anal intercourse was what God really intended then that was good enough for me – in theory, you understand.

Before service each day the KPs (kitchen porters) did veg prep for Archie the permanently soused veggie chef, the one with prison ink up either arm. They would sit askew on crates and peel carrots or onions, maybe run bags of spuds through the peeler and then nip the eyes off – this was their very own little world within a world, a veritable haven from the lives they led when the kitchen doors closed each night.

Outside, they would roam the streets or go back to their patch, dossing in the alley around back with the blessing of management as it's always better to have your own bums in situ rather than run the risk of having to eject boozeheads who you don't know. Every morning around three they would stand in the alleyway yelling, and after they got no response they'd clamber up the fire escape and lean around to bang on your window demanding you go down to the kitchen and fry them up a batch of hot chips. Yeah right, as if new apprentices could even turn a deep fryer on let alone rustle up a basketful of fries! Most of us hadn't even been allowed to use the electric kettle at home thanks to our old man's paranoia that we'd burn the damned house down. Anyhow you grew accustomed to their serenades, and after a while you didn't even hear them, so deeply unconscious were you in the Land of Nod.

Little John was the head KP and holding such a position of responsibility had obviously gone to his head. Each morning he'd go through the pantomime routine of inspecting his fellow KPs to ensure they were all shipshape and Bristol fashion. There they'd all be lined up like the cast of *It Ain't Half Hot Mum*, holding mops with shiny buckets at their usually shoeless feet while Little John walked up and down with that serial-killer smile etched on his ruby-red lips. It was a bizarre sight: old Harold straight from a night in a cardboard box standing there in his op shop pants three sizes too big with his wrinkled old pecker poking through his fly because he's got no underwear; Mr Henry (surname unknown) who was once a desert rat, but was now just vermin, standing there hardly able to remain upright as the lack of booze brought on his vertigo again; and McTavish, who wasn't even really Scottish but claimed to be a Laird who'd renounced his wealth and titles for a life of scrubbing copper pots until they shone so much that he could see the family resemblance to William Wallace in them. A more motley crew you couldn't wish to meet – but they were *our* crew, our KPs, the very people without whom the big kitchen would grind to a shuddering halt.

The KPs do everything. They run bets, fetch beer, mop floors, unpack dry store deliveries, scramble from section to section dodging flying pans and blue abuse. Once you get on first name terms and, more importantly, learn to respect your KP higher than any freaking waiter or food and beverage trainee, your KP becomes like a sherpa on the climb up

Everest. Once you've earned his respect, your KP can be trusted to set up your section if you know you're going to have a hot night on the sauce. Most section chefs will trust a KP they respect more than they'll trust some greasy-skinned apprentice. KPs have no ambitions beyond making it to the next payday without fully sobering up.

Even after you're yanked upstairs to do your time you still find a few minutes at the start of each shift to catch up with your vagrant co-workers. You demonstrate a genuine interest in their sordid affairs and, in return, when you need a basket of peeled and sliced carrots to save your life your KP will be there holding the goods and your arse will be spared a good booting. Run out of sauté pans mid service? If you're the type of dick-head who thinks that the pot washer is just another disposable commodity, then don't expect a stack of clean pans to appear miraculously on your station. Forgotten how to prep an artichoke even though you've been shown twice already? No worries, nip downstairs for another impromptu lesson from your KP and then later, over-order on the lunchtime booze tab and send three pints down to the prep area on the dumb waiter. There are ways my friends and there are ways – and while there might be a hundred ways to skin a cat, believe you me: there's only one fucking way to prep an artichoke or turn a mushroom.

Your plonger, your KP, your dish pig, or later, as times changed, your dish bitch, are like good soil. Tended carefully it will grow great things. I learned that, I learned the most fundamental lesson on the pot wash – and that, shit for brains, as they say in the trade, is exactly why they send you down there! So stop your goddamned bitchin' and get polishin'.

So I did, and then the call came to go upstairs.

The brigade were all staring at me hard, the same stare death-row inmates give to fresh meat walking the landing buck-naked. Me though, I didn't look away – that's a big mistake, sister. I'd done my time slopping out, and now I wanted to caress the Big Time.

When you finally resurface into the maddening world above, where every goddamned thing whirs at a hundred miles an hour and no quarter is asked nor given, of course you can be forgiven for being somewhat out of kilter with life overhead. You have, after all, spent four blissful, if not at times dangerous, weeks living below ground with the alcoholics and sex fiends, and your flesh has taken on an unnaturally unhealthy hue usually associated with the onset of rigor mortis.

Your eyes have adjusted to the dimness of the enclaves and your mind has begun slowly but surely to resemble that great but maligned English staple called brawn. Your hands and feet are permanently wrinkled from hours on end stuck in rancid, larvae-infested swamp water. The hotel medico, Dr Mengeles, is amazed to see another case of trench foot and is excited by the prospect of yet more nocturnal experimentation on the company tab. Your sense of smell has quit for a fortnight in the Bahamas to avoid having to smell rotting pig bins and regurgitated seafood ever again.

Frankly, kid, you're a mess, and that's exactly what the first station chef to get hold of your pock-marked body as cheap labour will say – in a sick and delighted kind of way.

5.

Sweet Little Rock 'n' Roller

And then they let you start using those knives your old man bought you, those weapons of mass destruction that to date you've only used as fencing equipment up in your room. Knives are the most important thing a chef owns either in or out of the kitchen; I have witnessed terrible punishments meted out to any apprentice foolhardy enough to pick up another chef's knife and start hacking away on some beef bones with it like he was chopping wood for a fire. You might be able to take a quick sip from another chef's beer if you're game, share toothbrushes, money, women and even cars – but not knives, buddy. Chefs fighting over knives with knives is a ghastly and frightening sight, a chef fired up on adrenaline and staff-priced booze is a very dangerous creature to behold, and watching two chefs slug it out on the line with the nearest weapons at hand – water jugs, skewers, meat hooks, cleavers, rolled-up pornographic materials and even branding pokers – is the closest you get to seeing a homicide until you actually witness the real event out in the back alley one Friday night.

The fact they even let apprentices haul around a wrap of knives was surprising seeing the only knife most kids had used was table cutlery – and some hadn't even used that. There's always your villain who's been running switchblades since he was nine, or your ex-football hooligan au fait with fashioning any harmless implement into a deadly weapon, but most of these spotty-faced kids were knife virgins. The first day you're allowed to take out the chopping knife and wield it around like a sabre, with no responsibility whatsoever for anyone else's eyesight, is just like losing your virginity, only more thrilling. Once you get that blade in your hand, you feel invincible, and many an over-the-hot-plate stoush is settled in favour of the person thrusting the knife. I mean, what does a waiter brandish, huh? A corkscrew and a pair of tongs at best, a clean serving cloth at worst – like, come off it man, there's no arguing with a sleep-deprived homicidal maniac waving a fifteen-inch carving knife in your face! Why is the waiter risking his life or facial features over something as puerile as whether Italy plays ugly football, anyhow?

Every fool knows the answer's a gimme.

Glory be to the blade. So what if when you first whip out that filleting knife you scar a Spanish sommelier for life? Shit in a sidecar, sommeliers are a dime a dozen on the mean streets of Barcelona. No, my friends, wield that blade with a gusto that sends a clear and well-defined message to every other headcase in sight: look out fools, now I'm armed! No sooner have you apologized to Miguel as he lays clutching his forever-vanished Mediterranean looks in bloodied hands on a St John's stretcher, than the real heavyweights of the brigade have wrestled you to the tiled floor like a SWAT team. When this first occurs do not be alarmed, or struggle, for struggling only ensures that some psychotic deviant masquerading as a cold larder chef will seize the opportunity to grab a handful of things from your personal grab bag. Things that were never intended to be grabbed by another man.

If you are lucky you will receive instruction on the protocols of carrying large and deadly blades around a busy environment, on how to clean and store your knives, and most importantly on how to sharpen them. If not, then you just learn the hard way, which more than likely will entail gutting some poor fucker too stupid to realize you are only just out of the schoolyard. And that is their fucking bad luck, huh? Filleting the toast master while accidentally running through the kitchen with a ten-inch chopping knife held directly out in front of you is just one of those things, you know? But trying to cut good-quality meat with a blade as flat as a well-made crepe is another event entirely. You can, of course, make the basic mistake of letting someone more skilled in the art manhandle your knives in the act of sharpening, and after that it's your goods and chattels that'll be next up for the handling procedure. A knife is just another appendage you know? A phallic symbol. There are many pitfalls in the code of the knife, many subtle ways, but above all the user must learn to hone the edge so that when said user slices through the top of his or her finger for the very first time, the cut is so clean and painless the user remains blissfully unaware of the deed until he or she inadvertently glances down and notices that the chopping board is bright red instead of green.

Ah, that first beautiful cut, that inaugural trip to the kitchen's first-aid box where no Band Aids can be found because the squash-playing chefs have nabbed them all for the grips on their racquets. You stand there admiring your own handiwork while the chef designated to patch you up slips off to the bar instead, and you find yourself back on the line with one throbbing finger wrapped in electrical tape. The pain, they tell you – those with that white scar tissue on every finger and the burn marks cavalcading up forearms like junkie's track marks –

will go away. The scar, however, is like a notch on a bedpost, it is a badge, a reminder of happy times and great deeds, the central event in a large tale to be used on those who follow.

See this baby, they tell you gleefully, holding up one crooked finger or pointing to a horrific-looking scar, I got this baby in the service to beat all services. Three hundred and counting and man did we bust our balls that fucking night. Right at the death I asked (insert nickname of long since quitted chef) to throw me my boner – just a quick slit on the mignon because those goons in the larder had lost it good and proper, just grabbed that fucker in mid air and BAM! Straight through here and out the other side like a fucking harpoon, and you know what?

Of course we know what, we can be sure that this nutcase telling the tale just yanked that boning knife straight out of his own palm, wiped the blade with his dirty rubber, slit the mignon deftly, filled it with prawn and banged it on the flattop into a smoking sauté pan while he plunged his wound into a bowl of lukewarm water where a few sprigs of wilted parsley doggy-paddled for life. The hero finished service, wiped down his section, drank eight beers, grabbed a pizza, then casually meandered over to emergency to have a dozen stitches inserted. Next morning he was back in the kitchen making reductions for the lunchtime shift.

These are the heroic tales we all want to spin – so that first cut, which as the saying goes is the deepest, is sure one to be treasured. Chefs, you see, those breeds who twirl knives like a cheerleader in Baton Rouge, are impervious to pain. Whether this stems from alcohol or other drugs has not yet been fully researched but let me tell you, I have seen some gut-churning sights – enough blood to jug a hare and enough bone to make a half decent estouffade. All that matters is the Buzz, baby.

You want to know, of course, about my first serious wound. I mean *wound* not nick. A nick is something you acquire that a plaster covers up and you get those as regularly as you get to make the bar run. No, I'm talking about wounds, and mine didn't arrive until some quite considerable time after I'd first started playing with knives. Regrettably, however, it wasn't to be one of those heroic yarns I could weave through services forever after. No sir, mine came through sheer stupidity and a lack of attention. There I was doing it hard on the fucking cold larder with a section chef who had only arrived two days earlier following a dishonourable discharge from the RAF. You know the guys I'm talking about – ex-jarheads with flashbacks from severe Agent Orange poisoning. The guy had one of those natty pencil-thin moustaches that were en vogue during the Battle of Britain, and some kind of mental disorder I couldn't quite pin down. Back then my diagnostic skills weren't as accurate as they are today, nowadays I can spot a nutter ten miles away.

Anyhow, at certain times of the year big hotels go through this recruiting and replacement blitz, due to having lost so many good men to better wonga, unwanted fatherhood, medical conditions and glamorous foreign travel opportunities. This is known as 'silly season' and you can bet your last Durex that during these crazy times you will turn up pie-eyed for work to find your new section chef still believes that he is living in Colditz. This was one of those days and some of the boys had warned me over breakfast that I was in for one bad motherfucker, that I ought to skip extra toast and get some fucking prep going because the new guy didn't know one end of a sirloin from the other. Ye gods, I cursed, as I trudged wearily up to the Duce's palatial mansion-cum-office to look into the big book where the Duce had scrawled the day's menu in scribble that looked to the outsider like a script by Crippen. Yeah, it was full of bad news for any fool unlucky enough to be rostered on the larder on a day like that, full of cuts to be cut and fish to be filleted and fucking oranges to be segmented – the full fucking Monty.

And there he was, fecken Baden Powell, all dollied up with no place to go, and already an hour behind with the prep. The second-year on the section with me was going hard at Dover soles like a washerwoman doing shit-soiled daks on a rock beside the Ganges, never even looked up, just grunted as I tied my apron. The new guy had never seen a real kitchen, what he'd seen was some navvy or galley or mess or whatever those fly-boys call it down at Friggin Hill, all he'd ever done was unpack fish fingers and slip processed cheese slices between burgers. I made a quick start on the trout because they were on lunch and not dinner, disemboweled two dozen in double quick and wiped the guts on my apron before I started taking the sinew off whole beef fillets. One quick glance at the clock and I got that sickly feeling in my guts: we wouldn't be ready for service, not by a long stretch of even the most fertile of imaginations. Jesus H. Christ, those headcases on the line were going to bust our balls like nuts in a cracker, I was going to meet myself at least a dozen times coming back from the line with handfuls of sliced fillet for stroganoffs, and the gammon steaks?

I winced as I heard the first dockets being screamed out with a banshee yell that meant the line knew damned well that we were so far in the crapper that only piping the U-bend would flush us out. It had to be five fucking gammon steaks too; not a goddamned trout in sight – I mean what kind of brain job pays good money to eat trout anyhow? The second-year had a look on his face that I knew only too well, the look you see on men about to undergo a lethal injection. I slipped the fifteen-inch carver from my roll like a bullfighter whipping out his cape, but without the Ole! just indignant resignation that I'd been lumped in with a complete fool. There he was vainly trying to keep a tab on the crescendo of dockets being barked out by writing all over the goddamned fridge door with permanent marker, Christ himself couldn't solve this dilemma because when the Duce saw that fucking fridge door he'd have a full-blown litter of pygmies. The second-year, whose name escapes me, was close to tears trying to decipher the child-like scribblings, while I just kept my ears open and tried as best I could to salvage my own dignity from the chili con carnage to come. Sometime real soon that egg-sucking dog of a sous chef would have to stride over to see for himself what the fuck was going down, and I wasn't intending to be the one he congratulated with a Glasgow handshake.

I grabbed the gammon leg and started slashing at it like Jack the fucking Ripper himself. What I'd done was a hack job, not lovely round steaks, and I hurried them over to the line only to be met by a stare of complete disgust from the third-year on the sauce section. What the fuck's that? Gammon steaks, five of, I answered. The sous pulled himself away from his beloved dockets and grabbed me by the collar, the gammon fell to the floor and the fish chef kicked them under the range with a leery smirk. I tried boyfully to explain I was under the sway of a complete dickhead who couldn't tell smoked salmon from smoked ham, but those guys weren't big on first-years insulting section chefs so I got myself a cauliflower ear and a tramp stamp just to be going on with. Back in the arena of doom, mercifully the second-year had cut five okay-looking steaks and was en route like a patriot missile. Hearing another order for three salmon steaks, instinctively I hauled the smiling fish from the sink, slopping briny water all over the show, and instantly chopped off two fillets before I realized I was using the incorrect tool for the job – Jesus, what a fucking morning. And then without looking, I quickly wiped the blade of the fifteen-incher on my tea towel, and all I felt was an exhilarating sting. Then I noticed red, copious amounts of red, running down my arm. In my haste and panic I'd cleaned my knife, blade up, and had run the tip of my thumb its full length. The incision had gone deep, right through, save for a few shreds of skin still hanging on gamely for grim life here and there. It was a cut to be cherished, for sure, but certainly not one to be noted in the annals.

I showed my wound to the second-year as he raced past me sporting flushed cheeks; he merely glimpsed at the blood and told me it was just a nick, for Christ's sake, so I carried on, coating everything I touched a warm shade of crimson until finally Biggles emerged from his coma. His mood had shifted like a continental plate. In Baden Powell's place was some sadistic bug-eyed desperado ready to crash 'n' burn. I showed him the wound and he told me there were eight avocado on order, did I know what an avocado looked like? I told him I was feeling weak, and he said he was too! In all the excitement of finally being gainfully employed again he'd forgotten to take his meds that morning, could I hold down things while he shot up to the chemist? It was mid service and we were knee-deep in unfulfilled orders, was he fucking serious? Hell yes, he told me, there were more important matters in life than fucking avocados. And off he went, whistling. Something like When Johnny Comes Marching Home Again, Hurrah, Hurrah . . .

I was feeling faint, god knows how much blood I'd lost. Finally I had no choice but to abandon ship like King Rat himself, and as I made a speedy exit I saw the second-year fall to his knees in despair. I made for the chief's office but as per he wasn't home. The rule was you had to wait outside even though the first-aid box was almost within touching distance, so I stood there feeling myself drifting from consciousness as the screams around me started to fade from my sensory field.

Reluctantly, given the punishment for those stupid enough to enter the Duce's mansion without invite, I stepped into the office trailing claret all over the shag pile and fumbled with the key on the St John's box. Yup, no fucking plasters! Exasperated, I slid down the wall ending in a crumpled heap, and there I stayed out of harm's way until a Good Samaritan took pity on me – goddamned, wouldn't you know that it just happened to be Little John, who was delivering a parcel of clean whites and Scandinavian naturist reading matter. Chefs are mean when riled, when another complete incompetent throws their section into chaos. But no matter how mean they were, not one of them fancied a serious rut with Little John. My attention to KP duty had paid a handsome bonus.

I was taken to the first-aid staff member on duty and from there to a back-room F&B office to sign a dozen disclaimers before they took me to casualty. At the hospital they put five stitches in it and a shot in my arse for good measure, then swathed my throbbing thumb in pristine white bandages – no work for a week, they said.

Yeah, you guessed it, I was back on shift that night wearing a rubber glove and trying to fillet halibut because the boss hadn't gotten over the fact that his office looked like a crime scene and that some deranged fool had scribbled gibberish over a pristine fridge door. My thumb took six months to heal properly without that prescribed due rest and attention; the second-year on shift with me that fateful day absconded to an island off the west coast of Scotland to become a lay preacher.

And believe me, I never cleaned any of my knife blades arse backwards ever again.

Some lessons you learn through experience. How to handle knives and pressure are two of them, never to trust anyone straight from the military is another, and never to stop when you've decided to run is good too. Other mishaps however will always catch you out in a big kitchen. Burns and scalds are two of many. But we will return to those bad-arsed eventualities later, my friends, for now we must go back in time again to the life of a first-year live-in apprentice in a swanky hotel.

6.

Mamma Mia

Where's me fooking pants? Billy was moaning. The laundry always screwed with Billy's mind, never once did I know that kid to get back what he'd sent. Most days Billy turned up for work looking as if he'd slept in the skip. But it wasn't his fault.

The hospitality industry is a simmering broth of miscreants and wastrels, all with an opportunist bent. That's what Clarke, the F&B manager, told me while he tried to sell me someone else's prescription drugs.

Really? I'd said rather innocently.

You'd better fucking believe it, he'd replied, then he'd scampered off to some meeting while I rummaged through his still-warm wallet.

He was right. No sooner do you put something down than it's vanished. David Copperfield would be hard pressed to make stuff disappear faster. It's not just a rule that strikes in the kitchen you understand.

Take our whites, for example. 'Whites' are the nickname given to the chef's uniform, your jacket, pants, apron, necktie and, in those heady days, the ubiquitous overly starched cotton chef's hat – the one responsible for so much premature balding. Ever wondered why most chefs are dome heads by the time they reach thirty? Look no further than the hat, my friends.

The laundry in a big hotel is a bunker full of housewifey women folding bed sheets all day long; this is their domain and woe betide any fool stupid enough to stir the ire of the dragoness in charge. She is a veteran of many campaigns and will have seen everything that paying guest, rock star or apprentice chef can do to what was previously a pristine white sheet, so hard that it took five days to break in.

You received your bedding allowance once a week between certain hours: those were the rules, and if you were unfortunate to be with a section chef who frankly didn't give a flying turd about the cleanliness of your bed linen, that was your tough titties. Not only must you have mastered the Klingon cloaking device to manage to disappear mid shift to retrieve your putrid linen, but you have to suffer the indignation of several old ladies holding it up under infra-red lighting for a full inspection and report on the condition of the returned linen.

With the laundry girls you rely solely on your good looks, adolescent charm and backbone.

Unfortunately these virtues barely cut the mustard, not when you're standing there red-faced while granite-like gargoyles are holding up your sheet that has been slashed, defecated on or liberally soaked in blood. The laundry is the goddamned forensic lab of the big hotel, the CSI.

It's a bad and ugly gig, to be sure, when a black tick is again placed beside your name in the book of shame, when you know full well that the very next time you have to take the elevator down to the steaming bowels of the hotel with a bundle of soiled bedding, you're likely to come back up with a parcel of old brown paper for linen.

Oh, it's you again is it, Master Bed Wetter?

I don't piss my own bed, lady, people piss in it for fun!

A likely tale I'm sure, maybe we oughtta give you nappies?

Yeah, and maybe I ought to . . .

What exactly?

Nothing, lady, can I have me clean sheets now or what?

One avenue of discourse between chef and laundry lady squares the ledger somewhat – and that is the curse of the missing whites. In those bygone days we live-in category A prisoners had to bundle up our dirty whites with string once a week and attach to the bundle a completed page of our laundry book, to show how many of each item we had enclosed to be out-laundered. Two days later you went back to the laundry to collect your clean gear and that's when the real fun always began.

Some people, unscrupulous people, will write down they've sent five jackets, for instance, when in fact they've only sent three, in the hope that they will indeed get the fraudulent amount back, saving themselves the cost of buying two more jackets. This ruse worked for a while until the laundry cottoned on to what was occurring and from that date on we had to take our dirty gear loose and bundle it up under the eagle-like glare of a frosty matron. Not until she had countersigned our laundry book could our stuff be forwarded out of house. The real drama came when we got our clean gear back all nicely folded and starched. Lord only knows how much lice-infested chef's gear that contracted laundry had to cope with each week, but fuck me if you didn't always get back some other creep's gear.

Either your returned pants would be too big or too small, too long or too short, or your jackets would be button-less and frayed to pieces, probably eighteen sizes too big with a faded name like 'Boner' or 'Hell Boy' crudely written on the label. It was a lucky week if your neckties even came back at all, given the brisk black-market trade in such apparel. Hats? Well, it would only be in the elevator while you're still getting dressed for shift that you realized you looked like a prize prick – there is *no* keeping a hat up that is three sizes too big. Staples sometimes work, until the chef sees you and goes off the deep end about the dangers of having sharp metal objects too close to your perilously thin cranium. The next morning you find yourself in a very long and disgruntled queue of grunts holding armfuls of uniform that aren't theirs, waiting to undergo the dreaded 'exchange or replace' procedure. Sometimes your luck is in and three goons ahead of you you see a pale face from the pastry clutching your gear like it was the key to life itself. Hope springs eternal – if only you can grab your rightful belongings from the unclaimed slush pile, the one that is guarded as fiercely as Checkpoint Charlie. Tug of wars sometimes eventuate, brutish affairs where some mongrel of a chef is yanking on one arm of a disputed garment while three coalminers' wives go at it on the other.

After the mandatory wait period you can go to the laundry and request a 'lost chit'. This valuable piece of paper entitles you, the bearer, to report to F&B and have credited to your next pay packet the replacement cost of one jacket or whatever – or if you are very unlucky, and indeed thoroughly non-circumspect when it comes to purchasing your own replacement uniforms, you will be handed a threadbare replacement item from the triple-bolted unclaimed property cupboard as recompense. It will say 'Tiny' in faded felt pen on the tag and the jacket will be large enough to host a bar mitzvah under. The other hotel departments, alas, are no more inviting than the laundry . . .

Here is the stillroom, so called because the large boiling water stills are located within its sanctuary. This is the domain of the waiting staff. You will find them crammed into this room from early morn to late night, making toast for breakfast, making fancy toast for service, polishing cutlery with silver dip, buffing crystal, folding intricate designs into pristine napkins, grooming themselves constantly and invariably talking in Spanish. This room always smells of cheap cologne and garlic and it is an abyss in the otherwise busy universe of the grand hotel. Here you will find the large dishwashing machines and those who toil over them like gay firemen on a full-steam engine, just waitin' for her to blow. Unlike the kitchen porters with their inebriated ways and their knee-deep sinks full of brown water, here in the upper echelons you will often find that most despised of casual kitchen worker, the 'student'. They flock from all over to the bright lights, from all parts of the Isles and from continental Europe in their quest for education and a hands-on feel for the English language and good Anglo-Saxon flesh.

Many of course leave disappointed, their aspirations and youthful exuberance beaten down by the grind of long hours studying and even longer hours at the sinks.

The foreign student suffers more than his native fellow slave. Not only must the foreign student stay the full course of his or her summer placement if he or she is to have the placement card ticked, but where the native can abscond to any other gig, the foreign student is tormented to the point of derangement. The kitchen is a juvenile place, a nursery if you will for the spread of disease, and once the young apprentice chef discovers there are persons lower on the food chain than even he, all kinds of wonderful opportunities suddenly present themselves. In summer in the stillroom we find Helga and Boris, Kurt and Josef, Pierre and Svetlana, all eager to please and thrilled to be engaging in real dialect with real English people – until they realize they cannot understand one damned word of what you say, for the English language taught abroad bears about as much relevance to the native dialect as menu French bears to French French. These poor foreigners far from their families and tutors find themselves bombarded by accented swear words and phraseology that can never be taught in the stuffy confines of a classroom.

So you can imagine, knowing as you do a little about the sardonic wiles of the English kitchen brigade, just how tumultuous an experience English-language placements can be for the under-prepared student from Bonn. Heaven knows what kind of reception these poor kids get when they return to their classrooms abroad brimming with colloquialisms and profanities insistent that it's proper English.

Adamant that a waiter is called a 'dickhead' in England and that food is called 'grub' or 'nosh' and that a 'plonker' is a well-educated toff.

Imagine if you can the look of frozen horror on the young foreign intern's face when he is first faced with a rabid and half-cut McTavish up from the bowels in search of a certain implement, how the ears of the foreigner are under attack from not only a learned Scottish brogue as thick as a haggis, but from some kind of bizarre lingo that McTavish himself has created over his many years of imprisonment. Ye gods, it takes the English apprentice six months to understand the McTavish way, so how on earth any Dutch student would know what a 'rubber fucker' is beggars belief – yes indeed, that's just McTavish looking for the sink plunger.

Others who periodically frequent the stillroom and the kitchen are the sorry specimens known as grunts, the all-powerful F&B trainees doing general hotel and catering certificates. There is a consensus among the brigade proper that these individuals merit the most heinous treatment, to be meted out without pity for the term of their natural life. There was a brief time when I considered the life of the apprentice chef to be the epitome of an existence not worth living – until I witnessed the barbarianism of life as an F&B trainee.

His name was Colin and he hailed from Yorkshire. Tetley they called him, after the tea, and that was about as far as the bonhomie reached. Not only did Tetley have an accent that reminded us all of the great divide, but he came into our midst full of that tyke bravado and surly indignation, a package not best suited to winning over a southern brigade. I remember the day I arrived in the kitchen to see Tetley standing there looking like a scarecrow in chef's clothing, brand new still-creased gear with a roll of inferior brand knives under one arm and a cocky smile smeared across his face like strawberry jam. Christ Almighty, I recall thinking, that poor bastard is in for the sorriest time of his life.

For a month, at least, our own worthless lives would be exceedingly simple compared to this poor wastrel's. Even Billy, a fellow northerner, didn't waste any sympathies on the birds-of-a-feather philosophy. Fook that crap, he told me, let the poor bastard fend for 'imself and maybe I'll get left a-fooking-lone!

Tetley drew a short straw on day one and he was never able to select a longer one thereafter. No matter what job he was half-doing or what section he was on, his life disintegrated into a ball of loose threads. So what if he got locked in the freezer without his pants for two hours? He came from Yorkshire, didn't he? So what if some smart arse made a brand out of coat hangers that said 'pussy' and tried to burn it onto Tetley's butt while three other goons held him down and crowed with laughter? So what if the silly sod was dumb enough to take a pre-heated plate from the spook on chow duty? And who really cared if his personal mail somehow became public property and half a dozen kitchen agony aunts took to writing to his beloved without his knowledge? That is just the way of the game, and it is all undertaken in the best possible taste.

They told me after, those who had a finger on the pulse of the grand hotel machinations, that Tetley's folks were considering suing the hotel for gross negligence seeing as how their beloved boy had returned to them a gibbering wreck and his betrothed had eloped with a North Sea fisherman's wife. What kind of sadistic rituals are you practising down there? they bellowed, and any one of us could have easily answered. We were practising the art of professional cookery, by The Book, as it were.

For all his bullheadedness and northern soul, poor Tetley never quite caught a hold of the very simple concept that not answering back can have a pacifying effect on a deranged chef demonstrating the first signs of Tourette syndrome.

Let us proceed up the flight of stairs to this small door, for here lies the most important room of all in the big hotel – the wages room, manned every Friday morning by those who dole out the pittances to the downtrodden and incarcerated. Once that small blue wage envelope is in your sticky little hands, you have to run the obstacle course, dodging and weaving through the line hoping to avoid all of the fellow crims you've borrowed beer or fag money from, and if you're lucky you'll make it back to the kitchen with enough bread for a couple of beers on Friday night. Yeah, payday, I've got days off on my mind. Even if you don't make it, there are plenty of cashed-up loan sharks with private slush funds willing to sub you at a generous rate of interest. Bruce was one such person, one of the very first of what became a tsunami of Antipodeans ready, willing and sometimes even able to pick up the slack in the British hospitality scene. And slackness there was after so many kids had seen the light and opted instead to night fill supermarket shelves or indulge in a twilight life of wanton crime and fuck the consequences.

Bruce the Australian, now there's a bad memory. That fly-by-night mongrel who commandeered the breakfast shift with an approach as sloppy and unhygienic as a cockroach on a smoked salmon platter. Bruce, with a glint in his eye, served food that vaguely resembled the great English breakfast, his big gold earring flashing under the fluorescents long before big gold earrings were the rage, his moustache hanging there draped over his top lip like a dead possum. Bruce, one of his many aliases, had travelled the world on merchant ships, or so he boasted; that was how he'd grown his amphibious legs and obtained his first-mate's cooking diploma. Ever tried knocking up a few eggs while you're going from forty-five degrees to forty-five degrees like a bloody pendulum, huh, cobber? Bruce was quick on the uptake, or so he reckoned, and to be sure he had quickly grasped the basic concepts that dictate live-in protocols in large hotels. He had learned, for instance, that the motley crew of chambermaids who trooped down for swill at some ungodly hour would willingly trade favours in the early yellow dawn of the new kitchen day; another piece of dried-up bacon here, an extra dollop of rubbery scrambled eggs there – well, you get the picture, I guess. Bruce had about 150 kids scattered around seaports the world over, a dynasty of evil little Bruces that would one day take over the world via the finest hotel kitchens.

Like all Australians, Bruce had a story for every occasion, from how he'd wrestled crocodiles in the tropics for grog money to how he had been personally involved in coups in jungle hellholes. Bruce liked you to know that he was a dangerous breed, not the kind of breakfast chef who took ridiculing of his egg cuisine lightly – hence the cow horns and machete that always adorned his station. Bruce chopped the potage vegetables with his machete and made the big-knife joke notorious long before Crocodile Dundee came to town.

This was not long after the movie *Jaws* had scared the bejesus out of everyone and even English beaches were deserted. I mean as if you ever saw a great white shark off the coast of Brighton? On the promenade perhaps but . . . hell yes. We swam at dawn and dusk and some mad bastards like that imbecile Bob would go under water and grab your ankle, or your balls. There was fear all right, a pandemic of edginess, even about paddling on a pebbly beach in the wee twilight hours. Bruce just laughed it off, called us all whinging poms and was always first into the cold grey sea, swimming out three miles as fast as a torpedo, naked to boot. Bruce liked to share his manhood with everyone. Off he'd go, leaving his shorts, flip-flops and egg-stained T-shirt discarded on the beach. Only natural then that we'd abscond with his gear and leave the sorry bastard to walk dripping wet and stark bollock naked the half mile to the hotel. Bob the biter even rang the police once to tell them there was a flasher on the beach who sounded Australian. Yes indeed, there are predators everywhere and it pays never to let your guard down, not even amongst your so-called comrades.

Bruce got to feed lunch to the ever-ravenous lasses too, slopping up anything from the fridges that was on the nose or off-colour, the more putrefied the better because a deep fryer cures all. He would stand there in his flip flops doling out ladle after ladle of grease-laden goo as he sang 'Waltzing Matilda' for the umpteenth time that day, while the ever-growing northern lassies, like turkeys on a farm, stood there in the chow line all misty-eyed daydreaming of a nice little beachside residence somewhere in the sun, with weekly family allowance benefits times five thrown in.

Twice a year the hotel bussed chambermaids down from some place too far north to comprehend as civilization, and invariably these girls were the stoniest-faced women you could ever want to meet. Crackin' lasses, eh? Billy would say, slicking back his thinning hair.

They made a good sack, however, and that was all that mattered, that and the fact they worked for nothing other than free communal board with one stained bath between fifty of them. At the changeover twice a year, half the girls would be pregnant and half the kitchen brigade would just vanish into that twilight world known as the professional cookery circuit never to be heard of again. Lord Lucans we called them.

You could safely wager, even with Pierre the concierge who gave terribly short odds, that come mid-season you'd be manning a section all by yourself because your section chef would be en route to some cushy number in the Bermuda triangle with full board and return vacation passes to Disneyland included in the package. Good chefs don't leave; they simply disappear.

Chambermaids and their dedicated quest for husbands are the major cause of this yearly flight of fancy. Everyone's in on the act, except apprentice chefs, who never sexually harrass anyone because they don't know how. Most apprentices are fresh from the teat and still think they're living at home. To apprentice chefs in big hotel kitchens a girl is a foreign species –

especially if that girl happens to be from some far-flung outpost of the union and has a mouth on her like a BB gun.

On Bruce's days off, we apprentices had to cook staff meals, and damn well serve them too. Ye gods, there are terrible things they make you do in the name of cookery, and the worst of these is serving up grub to those entitled to a feed on the house. Apprentices are the very last people in an industrial kitchen you want to be fed by. Not only haven't they acquired even the most rudimentary knowledge of hygiene procedures and food re-heating techniques, but for the love of Christ, apprentice chefs can kill people! But more on that later as now I want to take you into the very private and dangerous world of the hotel porter. If, that is, you've the stomach for it.

7.

The Dark Side Of The Moon

After some undefined period of time hermetically sealed in the confines of the great hotel you are called to a manager's office for a wee chat. This affair is known as the 'Inquisition' and it is where you and your fellow inmate are interrogated for a half hour or so over various aspects of your tenure. Points such as whether you are enjoying the job, do you get on with your fellow primates, are the living conditions tolerable, et cetera. The one verboten topic is the rate of pay – start blabbering on about that and the weasel-faced person opposite will slyly feel under the desk for the security alarm, and next you know your accommodation will have been downgraded to a skip.

These little reviews, these cozy one-on-one chats, are meant not only to determine your state of mind, but to establish whether or not you or your bosom buddy are for turning; whether management can gain an insight into the sordid world that turns before their very eyes but somehow they constantly fail to see.

Of course, no one in the history of chef apprenticeships has ever been favourably cajoled toward the dark side. There is nothing any manager could offer by way of enticement that would alleviate the day-to-day flaying such a grass would endure.

The manager interviewing you will slip snippets he has gleaned into the conversation. He would be interested, for instance, to know a little more about the harmless fun that apparently takes place late at night in the ballroom? You, naturally, know nothing about such activities, nor anything about the rump steaks mysteriously vanishing from the cold larder. You sit there dumb-faced and tight-lipped striving not to utter one word that will incriminate anyone. All the while you know the ballroom is accessible from a small side door to which the older apprentices have fashioned a key from a block of lard, and that once five or ten of you are inside that huge room with its highly polished wooden floor there begins a wild nocturnal game of five-a-side football played frenetically by off-duty chefs in socks, the ball fashioned from the foam that fruit arrives wrapped in. You know also that under the stage in said ballroom is a corridor that leads to the dry store in the kitchen – a thousand mice can't be wrong, as the Chinese proverb goes – and no sooner are you in the dry store than it is simply a matter of hoping that the last slack-jaw to leave the kitchen didn't realize that the door wasn't locked. And then you are in, as they say in the trade, free to rustle up a half dozen rumps with fried eggs on top. All in all it is a good life, a life of hard work for sure, but a life full of compensations. Even the porters, those most feared of predators, can be bent to your will, for what is a hotel porter after all if not an opportunist, a snake, and as bent as a nine bob note? They, the porters, hold all of the keys to Babylon, and they may venture where'er they wish in the name of duty. But porters have one Achilles heel, and that fatal flaw is food.

The porter's army marches on its stomach, for this fine body of men is to the large hotel what the Republican Guard was to Saddam Hussein. The good porter knows as much about the workings of a grandiose establishment as a London cabbie does of London – for there is nothing untoward that can occur at any hour of the day or night in the big hotel that the porter does not hear or see. His is a world of habitual movement and of stealth, of wandering corridors in the pitch of night and listening at doors like an SAS paratrooper. When not engaged in these subterfuges porters are manning all entrances or relaxing in their secret abode, a room like the inner sanctum of a freemasonry hall, the 'lounge' as it is called. They are men, of course, who are beyond reproach, men who always recognize immediately a situation likely to cause distress to the paying patron, men ready, willing and able to assist any lady in even the inaugural throes of distress, and men above all others in the shitpit that is the human resources of the hotel, who can be trusted not only in a crisis, but indeed with that most cherished of big hotel idioms – the secret.

The hotel porter, privy to the woes and foibles of every member of the live-in staff after seeing them day in and night out in every situation, is a man who can be relied upon not to abuse the transgressor's trust. A good porter is not a stickler for the myriad of petty rules enforced on live-in personnel. He is the man you need to feed. This is the only proven route to personal safety, the only method whereby, provided you have not committed an obvious homicide in full view of the porter (and even then a porter may still find a way to disentangle you from such a mess), you can survive. The porter can be trusted to smooth out those tiny wrinkles that sometimes threaten the otherwise flat millpond of your abidance.

Absolutely shitfaced and still wandering the streets like a bum at four in the morning when you're supposed to be on breakfast shift in an hour? Have no fear, the porter will dispatch someone to locate you and will have the coffee ready by the time you are carried back. No longer want to be hassled by that grim-faced girl you met last Friday night at some badly lit club? Worry not; the porter will see her away with a couple of bob for cab fare. Run short of alcohol, drugs, or pornography? Look no further than the porter's lounge, amigos. Need a clean shirt and a tie for your forthcoming court appearance, tickets for the big game, an alibi? Need a small superficial wound sutured to avoid an emergency room inquisition, a shot of penicillin, anti-fungal cream for that rash in an indelicate place? Well, you know who to call. Aladdin had nothing worth having in his cave compared to what the average porter has stowed in his, the Tardis he travels in: car jacks, pick axes, sporting equipment, small portable generators. That species known as the night porter has its fingers on many pulses simultaneously, much like Shipman; this is the reason why night porters and chefs in all hotels will always be found flocking together.

For while the day porters may eat staff food, most night porters prefer their victuals a little more edible. Even though they enjoy unrestricted access to the kitchen during their patrols, most decide not to rummage through the coldrooms and shelves looking for gourmand nibbles. What they are left by the good people of the kitchen is a platter known as the 'night porter's tray'.

Depending on the relationship between porter and the person charged with the making up of the tray, who knows what might turn up? I have seen night porter's trays that look so rank that a skip-diver would turn his nose up at them, and trays that look so bountiful they might have been prepared for a late-arriving head of state: shrimp, lobster, stilton cheese, smoked trout, chocolate éclairs, to name but a few of the goodies. And once the porter develops extravagant taste buds, bread and cheese sandwiches never hold the same allure. The porter is a bought man, bought and paid for on a nightly basis, just like having an inside man on a bank job or a direct route to Stalin himself. So please remember, next time you are departing a swanky hotel muttering about the scandalous over-charging, to tip the porter. They are the grist of the big hotel's mill.

Rudi was one such porter, and that much was confirmed in his obituary. Deaths are messy events for the big hotel. No place wants to acquire a reputation for strange deaths unless those strange deaths feature a rock star very prominently – in which case they are every big hotel owner's dream.

Rudi had won himself a reputation as 'Mr Dope', the kind of person who fits into the greater scheme of things like cheese and chives atop a baked potato. Except that one day Rudi was the life and soul of the eternal party, and the next plenty of chefs were celebrating because their credit lines wouldn't have to be repaid. No one really knew anything – apart from the other porters, who of course knew everything. Rudi had OD'd on some bad shit, they said knowingly, they'd found him slumped over a toilet in a bathroom on the third floor. (Actually it would later be proven that he suffered an aneurysm while trying, straining, to break his bad run of constipation.) The porter who discovered Rudi and thus circumvented what could have been a very sticky situation if some guest found the poor bastard slumped there like one of Nilsen's fresh kills, got awarded a bronze star and a week at the company's grand Blackpool hotel with a twilight tour of the illuminations chucked in.

Rumours buzz around big hotels like flies over a still-warm corpse. Before you knew it, poor old Rudi had a hundred tales to his posthumous name. Life settled down awhile until early one morning there was all kinds of hullabaloo after some chambermaids went into that very same bathroom to give it its daily once over, only to find Rudi slumped over the toilet bowl again, like he'd just had a bad vindaloo. Those lasses were pretty smartly put on a bus to Jarrow or someplace and nowt more was said of it apart from in the staff quarters ... where believe you me a lot of stuff, most of it bullshit, is spoken by the disgruntled.

But the weird sightings kept on until even the guests got wind of the haunted bathroom affair and management became edgy enough to start roaming the corridors at night in menacing pairs. Some of us live-in chefs used to go down there very early in the morning to catch a glimpse of old Rudi too, but by Jesus if we had ... no sir, that gig is not for me. The chambermaids were into it, though, they're paid to be, and before you know it Rudi had taken to walking the third-floor corridors looking for a fix or an enema and howling like a mad dog at midnight.

This caused more problems, seeing as how no chambermaids would go near the third floor after that, and in those days there weren't no such thing as folks who get paid to see dead spirits off to their designated destination. In the end, faced with either completely renovating the entire third floor and maybe turning that bathroom into a linen closet, or sacking every chambermaid on some flimsy pretext, management of course took the hard money option and bussed all of those gals right back to the Black Country. That'd fix it for sure, only it didn't, because no sooner had a new crew arrived than some ashen-faced northern lass almost had a coronary after seeing a man slumped over a toilet in the third-floor bathroom early one morning, and when she asked him if he needed help he ... makes me quiver it does, just thinking about it. I see enough spooks on the line, thanks, without havin' to go searching for them in the toe-curling hours.

In the big white world there's always something happening, new people arriving, from everywhere.

8.

Yes Sir, I Can Boogie

There's a Frog in the kitchen now, Billy told me after I'd returned from a weekend home.

Wow, that'll liven things up, eh?

Billy just shrugged. He was no Europhile.

Gyson was his name, pronounced Gee-son. He was of that special breed of Gallic men, those booze-ravaged chefs who not even the most provincial of provincial kitchens in France would take a chance on any longer. The type of waxing-lyrical scumbags who are literal fucking galloping gourmets and drink like sperm whales. Gyson and men like him drifted from their native shores like William the Conqueror harbouring notions of again subjugating the English.

In every kitchen the breadth of the land you will find a man much like Gyson huddled over a steaming pot of gruel. You will recognize him instantly – a man with his laughing gear permanently attached to a liquor bottle. Of course, no sooner have these men crossed the Channel than they become born-again gourmands preaching to the philistines – to be sure, Gyson and his cronies considered English fare lower than a pregnant sow's belly.

You would find him every night in his small corner of the

abyss muttering to himself in street French while he stirred the pot, all the pots actually if we're talking literally – and Gyson, let me tell you right now, guarded his broth with that ferocity only a Frenchman can muster, even while he flinched foodstuffs other less gourmand nationalities treat as vermin and kill with baits and traps.

By service time Gyson would be ripped to the tits on cheap speed and gin, bawling out the 'Marseillaise' with a gusto that hasn't been heard since the guillotine last sped groundwards, doling out his specialties de la maison for all to marvel at, and waving his ladle like a baton until all the stew had vanished.

After such nightly exertions Gyson would bid us a cheery adieu, leaving his demi-section looking as if it had just been plundered by Blackbeard himself, then retire to the more comfortable surroundings of the bar, where he'd regale those willing to listen with the story of the bouillabaisse. How his long-gone mama had made the dish famous along the wharves of Toulouse or some place, and how he, Gyson, had been handed the treasured recipe as a chalice he should carry through life.

He's a fooking headcase, Billy told me. Tried to get his paws on me kit he did, the Frog bastard.

Gyson was as mad as it is possible to be and still remain at liberty. By his own account he had been on the run from the Legion since he was twenty and had spent his entire life thereafter plying his one and only ware at any restaurant that would hire him from Calais to Cairo. Gyson was the quintessential one-trick pony; but so long as the pony's trick is great, who really cares?

While management huddled around a backroom table someplace having orgasms over Gyson's broth, the man himself would be looting the bar of as much gin as he could haul – which was a lot. Whereas other chefs in the brigade were expected to prep their sections for both lunch and dinner, dear old Gyson poured Gallic disdain on the lunch hour as merely a time when the uneducated and slothful eat. The great man would arrive sometime around three each afternoon while the kitchen was in flux and begin to go through his well-rehearsed and top-secret routine. By the time the brigade started to drift back in for the evening service Gyson would have ransacked everyone's prep, leaving a trail of shellfish from the larder to his cozy nook. With a guttural curse of *merde*, Gyson would discard much of what he selected for his stew, all the while lamenting the poor quality of English foodstuffs and the blandness of the fish stock. The situation got so bad that a few chefs began taking their prep with them on their afternoon siestas, and when you've catnapped with a dozen lobsters, as they're fond of saying in Mafia circles, you've slept with da fishes.

Gyson, however, was a proud man, and like all proud men he had fallen many times. The last time he fell, the plastered bastard never got back up again – and chefs being chefs, there occurred an undignified scrimmage around the unconscious Frenchman while frantic white-jacketed henchmen rifled his pockets for loose change and the famous recipe. This is what chefs are like, and many events seem to spark these heinous scenes, although the biggest scene seems always to be reserved for the bouillabaisse recipe – and why not? The dish is a classic, and once you have found a recipe, a genuine heirloom, you are far better off than either Jack Hawkins or Long John Silver ever were.

9.

Do You Wanna Be In My Gang?

Back then, we apprentices merely watched such scenes bug-eyed. It was just a recipe after all, and yes, we were young and foolish, still basking in the resonant glow of even the most minor of successes. The seventies was a happy and hot time, when old people sat sucking on ice creams while they listened to the Sally Army band strike up a stirring rendition of, well, something stirring, I guess.

A time when families thronged to the beaches and spent long hours diving off sewage outlets into murky water, and many more hours sitting in casualty departments from the consequences. An era when English hotel guests were just becoming au fait with the sophisticated trend of late dining, and a time when the humble pork pie eaten on the prom was the first sign of the alfresco craze to come. Yeah well, I for one was quite content with the English system, thanks, it had served us well through many times, times of crises and of peace and tranquility. Even Francis Drake had managed to get home in time for tea, and I saw no logical reason why people couldn't get their fat arses up off the beach towel at four o'clock and be ready for swill at five thirty. Chefs have lives too, you know!

Okay, so it's not much of one, granted, but if they were going to insist (as they did back then) that the pub close at some ludicrous hour of the night like nine thirty, how in the hell was the poor chef going to be able to drink himself legless if hotel dining trends grew later? These were conundrums that better men than I wrestled with after hours in smoke-filled back bars. One school of thought was the 'fuck them all' school, and I had hitched myself to that particular rum-sodden wagon. Hell, apprentices already had late room-service orders to attend to twice a week, and if English people suddenly believed they had more in common with Lisbon than Leicester things were bad. The other, more progressive school of thought, adopted mainly by hotel owners and accountants, was all for heralding in a new and prosperous era of midnight dining. Ye gods, this is exactly why people quit hospitality!

Eventually, however, we had to meet the demand – after all we are professionals and as such we must live and die by the knife and the last-order docket . . . The Book says as much.

From this dilemma sprouted the seedlings of my disenchantment with people who insist on pushing last-order rules to the limit. To be sure there is always some half-cut fool with a loose woman of the night draped over one arm and a menu over the other who believes that the kitchen should/will/can/fucking well ought to serve him food. Of course, no sooner has the attending waiter thrown centuries of custom out the window in a vain quest to appease some F&B trainee with designs on promotion, than we are all in a stinking mess. Who benefits? we chefs often ponder over a joint. Not the hotel – how much do you think it costs to keep the lights blaring and the grills burning, just to feed one ginhead with a grudge against tradition? And aren't these latecomers so often the most obnoxious pig-headed cretins that any chef could hope to feed? Yes they are, for no late diner ever says thank you or leaves a tip. These people are like wolverines, crawling about low on all fours, their bellies dragging along the ground, hanging around posh hotel entrances just waiting for the opportunity to impress the kind of woman who charges by the quarter hour.

It will invariably take them a half hour to order wine, and then a further half hour or more to study the menu as if they were fucking Romanoff himself. Then, by god, they will have the barefaced gall to ask what the specials are. SPECIALS! the irate and red-eyed chef unlucky enough to have drawn the short straw will scream, ARE YOU FUCKING INSANE, MANUEL! This is not a query about Manuel's mental health, of course, this is a statement, and Manuel will scuttle back to his shitfaced customer full of humble apologies, which naturally will include a gratis cheese platter. By this stage tensions in the kitchen have passed boiling point and many filthy words are being used to describe the late patron. Sometimes a manager might venture into the blue-aired kitchen in a useless attempt to alleviate the situation with a frivolous comment or some weak-livered tale about the late motherfucker being a 'regular'. Well yes, indeed, if he was he'd know damned well not to piss off the chef, wouldn't he? No regular in their right mind eats at fucking ten forty five in the p.m., regulars are fully aware that the best grub arrives early and after that it's downhill all the way like a hot turd in a U-bend.

But no, this terrible curse continues to feed on the good-hearted and thorough professionalism of chefs like an incurable disease. We can safely wager that the late patron will not be happy with steak and chips, no sir, this fucker will want nibbles, soup, a fish course, a main with tossed fucking salad and a side of dauphine potatoes, a half hour rest between courses and a dessert and cheese platter to boot. Why is this? No one knows, but I can tell you that of all the bad and terrible creatures that stalk a professional chef day in and day out, the late diner stands proudly erect at number one.

Many years after my training had finished and I was still being paid a pittance by some pretentious five-star hotel, I had the misfortune to find myself one of several lippy staff 'kept back' to service the requirements of a late-arriving foreign head of state or someone equally as appalling. High-class hookers would have sufficed, and indeed were in plentiful supply in a secret room adjacent to the on-duty F&B director, but alas these kinds of political types get a sadistic kick out of picking the bones of service industry workers clean.

So there we were, three of us, standing around with little more to do than play pocket billiards while we awaited the imminent arrival of old Henry 'kiss 'n' tell' Kissinger himself. An hour passed and the soup had reduced to a thick glaze. Top that fucker up with bain water, the duty chef told me angrily, his temperament not the kind that accommodated the fickle whims of American secretaries of state. After some considerable time had elapsed there was a sudden and quite unexpected rush of activity and without any warning we were surrounded by bubble-gum-chewing SS men intent on strip searches. Some kind of unpleasant incident followed whereby the section chef was maced, then dragged off to the dry store to be anally examined. Upon his return he was fully compliant with directives as the F&B men made hurried notes in little black books, jotting down reminders like 'order mace', I presume.

Afterwards everyone regained some degree of composure and an uneasy truce was bargained – we would feed HenryK whatever he fucking pleased until whatever time he pleased and in return the SS wouldn't make us play Russian roulette just for kicks. Jesus fucking Christ Almighty, just what kind of a low-rent gig had I signed up for? Don't worry kid, one of the sunglass-wearing men in black said to me, you'll get a real kick out of feeding HenryK, they all do, and then the guy proceeded to laugh so much that he almost croaked it there and then.

The other guys in the posse told us HenryK was world renowned for having a ravenous appetite and that we'd better start rustling up some more food, perhaps sling a full tenderloin or two on the grill just to be going on with? And keep 'em rare boys, coz HenryK loves 'em oozing. Ye fucking gods, there we were running around under martial law while a dozen SS sucked crab claws dry and threw the empty shells into the watery chowder for extra flavour. These boys had already laid off the waiting staff for the night: HenryK doesn't like young boys to watch him eat they told us menacingly as they re-arranged the restaurant to accommodate the boss. Although that's not to say that he's averse to young boys generally, understand?

All we need is one of 'em serving spoons for the chowder, they told me, pointing to a No 16 soup ladle, the rest HenryK'll polish off with his fingers. The guy likes to feel his food, see?

Yeah, I saw all right, HenryK was a bona fide connoisseur of many fine pleasures, and that explained why at two in the damned morning we were prepping up a couple of Wellingtons just in case.

Finally the big guy arrived and, surrounded by two dozen men in black disguised as sommeliers, fussed about the heaving table with a delicate dignity. Out on the Channel sat two US warships with lights blaring and missiles unlocked just in case some winehead got too friendly with the 'chief'. All of this hoo ha and protocol to feed one man – and you know what HenryK finally chose? Two slices of skinless chicken breast and a small spoonful of potato salad, and then he grabbed up five hookers, a free house kimono, a dozen Cuban cigars, two bottles of cognac, three attaché cases and a slab of Gruyere cheese and simply vanished into the abyss of the hotel night never to be seen again – much like the five hookers. So much for latecomers, huh?

There are many such sordid tales in the jungle – like the time I was taking spit-roasted ducks off the spit bar in the foyer of a swanky French riverside restaurant. It was a re-enactment of the court of Henry VIII as two of us sat baking in front of the roaring flames watching the spit turn. It was a cozy gig, for by this juncture in the saga of professional cookery swans, oxen and wild boar had all but been outlawed from the spit. Ducks aren't heavy, dead or alive. Anyhow, a well-known DJ and television comedian burst into the foyer with a madam tied tight around his neck but no tie. The madam was acceptable, naturally, but the Catalan maître d' refused to budge on the tie issue. A fracas developed when the B-list celebrity waved away the house ties kept for such situations, and both the comedian and the Catalan ended up rolling on the floor while the madam stomped the poor Spaniard with eight-inch stilettos like he was a paying client. At one point she even had the temerity to order another gin sling and casually return to the fray. Chefs become accustomed to turning a blind eye, especially when they are in charge of roasting forty ducks.

Another time a well-known US actor starring in a hugely popular detective show got into a messy scene with a homicidal junkie from the pastry in the service elevator and a host of suits had to club the offender half to death with Moet empties.

Chefs, you see, are a law unto themselves, even rock stars in the kitchen don't rate much of a distraction – not when you've a stock to reduce. The Book is adamant on such points and The Book is always right. But first to college …

10.

School's Out

We would have to leave the nest eventually and after twelve months of only being allowed to speak to immediate relatives on a monitored 'line', that inevitable and legally required time had finally arrived. The Duce summoned Billy and me to his office and sat there dreamily telling us about his school days in Burma as he sipped from the new batch of poteen the Lost Boys had whipped up from spud skins. His eyes grew heavy with moisture and his moustache twitched like a dying fox, and the posture he'd adopted only accentuated his man boobs. Jesus H. I hope I never got those kinda things . . .

Are you listening to me Luiz, you little fuck? he asked endearingly.

Sure boss, I replied, but those bitch tits just wouldn't leave my field of vision.

We would be temporarily leaving his care for eight weeks of intensive Mon–Fri tuition at the local college; the hotel expected us to uphold its envious reputation for churning out students well-versed in the arts of professional cookery and heavy drinking, and at all times to bear in mind that we weren't just 'any' chefs, we were chefs from a big hotel with big ambitions and a BIG name.

Yeah, well, fuck that bollocks, Will and Ben told us, being at college is a way cushy gig, like having eight weeks' paid vacation. You're surrounded by purring hot pussy in the reception school and a load of spacks from other hotels who have only just grappled with the basic principles of potato peeling. All you have to worry about is Mr Jean Paul the head of the hotel department, that fucker'll have it in for you right from day one just because you're following after us – and boys, we made that Frog's life a living hell, check out if he's still got that facial twitch we gave him, huh!

Yeah, great, I remember thinking, this is just the kind of gig I need, eight weeks under the supervision of a sadistic Frenchman with a cleaver or two to grind.

Don't worry about that fucker anyway, the lads told us confidently, what you don't wanna be is the first moron to speak out of turn, right?

Right, we said.

Because Jean Paul Buhmiester despises cretins who make fun of his name. There's always one smart mouth, one fucking idiot who'll say something witty, and that poor bastard has about as much chance of qualifying as Billy there does of getting a half-decent blow in the lunch break!

I bet there'll be some crackin' lasses there, eh? Billy asked me, and I was sure there would be – but none willing to pop Billy's cherry, I had bets on that.

On Monday Billy and me walked up through town together carrying our pristine whites. Well, mine were pristine, but Billy was still deep in some kind of laundry dispute and his were best described as browns. We were like playtime buddies on the first day at primary school. How strange was it to be out in the real world if only for an hour? At the school a curt and grumpy woman with blue hair directed us down to a basement. She had seen it all before, and plenty more besides. In the dungeon we were suddenly bombarded with a thousand questions by thirty-odd apprentice chefs in various states of disarray and nervous anticipation. One kid was stood on another's back peering through the grate while he gave a running commentary on scores out of ten for the legs of wannabe receptionists making their way down to the typewriting school.

Any crackin' pins, mate? I heard Billy say.

The other kid's name was Jay and he was already a sex addict and hardened drug-taker. No sooner was he down off his makeshift perch than he was trying to flog good quality Dutch weed that his sous chef brought back from visits to brothel land. Despite the generous percentage off to others in the trade, Billy and me declined his kindly offer. Initially, at least, we were there to shine.

In reception we sat in pairs all togged up awaiting the arrival of the eminent head of the cookery school, and while waiting we had to fill in forms that asked us about our sexual practices, known diseases, place of previous incarceration et cetera, plus a battery of documents that had to be signed to exonerate the school from any liability vis-à-vis serious bodily harm, degenerate liver diseases, mental incapacity, or complete nervous system failure that might befall us.

After this, a robust young woman with a savagely low-cut top and wanton demeanour swung her hips among us while prick-teasingly collecting up the forms. Then the great man himself arrived like Hitler entering the Munich Beer Hall, took a seat on the stool in front of us, and studied the forms while his face twitched. Finally he handed the forms to his buxom PA, sighed wearily, composed himself, and began.

The Frenchy's speech was, word for fucking word, just like the lads had told us, or indeed, verbatim as the girls liked to say after one morning in Miss Wetherby's highly regarded 'typing for unnatural blondes' class. After Monsieur Jean had finished his stirring reveille, there descended a moment's silence when all appeared well ... until the big dumb brute from another joint spoke up, Uh, Mr Bumfucker, I don't get the part ...

CHEF! YES, CHEF! Jean Paul shrieked crazily like Napoleon himself, and then two goons subdued the meathead and dragged him away for re-education.

Anyone else please, do speak up now ghentlemens? Non, voilà, and then let us begin!

CHEF! YES, CHEF! the rest of us yelled in unison.

The able-bodied PA's name was Miss Jenkins, and she held the lofty rank of school-nurse-cum-secretary-to-the-great-man. Yes indeed, Miss J waltzed around with an unbridled abandon and a sartorial style associated with street walkers; some days she was only barely dressed and other days she was barely dressed at all, it was a fine line. Will and Ben had already filled our minds with anecdotes from their time at school, and man, Miss J had a mouth as sweet and silky as a ripe ogen melon and a tongue as eager as an adder's on the first day of spring. Yeah well, that might be so, but at this school I was hell bent on learning something that might come in useful one day that didn't involve a set of skeleton keys.

The boys swooned over the tempestuous Miss J in the way young boys free of parental guidance and already well on the road to promiscuity are prone to swoon. Many self-inflicted near-fatal wounds on themselves so they could lay there dizzy with swollen glands in the sick bay, for it was rumoured that Miss J enjoyed sucking young chefs' blood – amongst many other suck-able things.

Some fell for Miss J in a bad and heavy way – especially

those who had suffered sheltered upbringings and long nights in rooms with mould-covered walls and just an old sticky *Playboy* magazine for company. A few returned from a prolonged visit to 'the Room', as it was known, with a swaggering bravado that conveyed Miss J had indeed relieved them of all that ailed them.

As I recall, young Billy finally succumbed to the inevitable one rainy afternoon when he came down with a bad case of swine fever and had no alternative but to visit the Room. I didn't see him again until after class, a delay that resulted in Billy never fully coming to grips with the concept of yeast bakery. Billy did tell me that night, however, completely off-the-record, that all Miss J did was take a quick shufty at his pecker, snigger girlfully and give him two aspirin and an old *Penthouse* to be going on with. These are the breaks, I'm afraid, and many nubile young men fell into the henhouse only to find far bigger foxes already on the game. And the biggest fox of all was old Golden Brown himself, our Legumes teacher.

This big, bearded ex-pirate could be found many a lunchtime in the local taverna leading boisterous renditions of such classics as 'Rule Britannia' and 'A Pirate's Life For Me'. By the time our class rolled around, old Golden Brown was as cut as a line of cheap cocaine and our tuition in the culinary preparation of fresh legumes suffered horrendously as a consequence. Golden Brown acquired his handle from his use of the much-heard phrase 'Get it golden brown boy!' – usually followed with a heavy clout to the incompetent's head.

Despite these odd routines and characters, most of us buckled down to a tedious life of textbooks, French culinary terms, butchery lessons conducted in sub-zero temperatures, afternoon lectures on the merits of shallow frying and goddamned menu planning. Intermittently we would break this monotony with a pint or two at a nearby alehouse, the Obedient Dachshund or some such, a haven for juvenile delinquency where elevated heels played a pivotal role in young men becoming fully-fledged alcoholics before their eighteenth birthday. But by five o'clock we were hauling arse through town to make the mandatory night service.

Back at school we were advancing well, although the repetitious collecting of exact quantities of ingredients from the old fool who guarded the dry stores was driving every fucker close to insanity. In our real kitchens if we wanted, say, tomato puree, then we just ripped open a catering-size can and slopped that mother all over the show, but at college if you needed tomato puree, which you invariably did, you could only obtain the precise amount designated by the recipe you were following. Say it called for one teaspoon of tomato puree, then off you'd go to Captain Beefheart with a teaspoon, and after shovelling as much onto the teaspoon as you could, the old sod would pare it off with a putty knife before allowing you to leave. Jesus H. this was no damned way to learn to cook – as I'd begun to understand during my extended lunchtimes at the Frisky Dachshund or whatever that place was called.

Jean Paul was by then developing Alzheimer's. Neither his memory nor temperament was as sound as in his glory days, or indeed gory days. Many a time he would have us perform the same meaningless task over again until that old fucker in the dry store popped another blood vessel. What this was achieving I still don't know.

And then there were the public restaurant duties every Monday, Wednesday and Friday, supposed 'real life' services to the great unwashed and finicky OAPs with free meal vouchers cut from the local rag. On Tuesdays and Thursdays we got to feed the students, and small wonder many withdrew from their studies after a severe bout of Mr Salmon Ella's tender lovin'. Yes indeed, those restaurant services began to take on a pantomime quality as Mr Jean Paul barked out orders and a platoon of retarded goons went through their child-like routines of branding each other with hot pokers, rubbing crushed peppercorns on their fingers then on the nearest person's lips, or coating another moron's station in apricot jam just for fun. Most of the time half of the cretins' prep wouldn't even be ready anyhow because their ovens/rings/grills had been turned off or down by other more savvy persons. Food was constantly being returned by the OAPs unhappy with raw roast potatoes and meat with more vital fluid than the Red Cross blood bank.

What in a normal kitchen would take thirty minutes, invariably took three goddamned hours in the hybrid world of the school restaurant – and even then some of the dupes still couldn't keep up. By the end of 'service', when stragglers from the blue-rinse set were struggling to finish the last of some stewed-to-buggery fruit with instant-set concrete on top, the whole kitchen looked like El Alamein and too many of our comrades had fallen. The two sorry-arsed saps designated to the sinks for that day's service would be close to tears as they peered, terrified, at a mound of copper burned black and an array of pans no longer distinguishable as cookery utensils.

After that sorry debacle we trudged off wearily to bakery looking like the Boche coming back from the front after another hard week in the trenches. For what remained of the day we would play with yeast goods, too afraid to take the designated break for coffee, pills or cigarettes in case some half-wasted miscreant might bang our oven door open and shut several times to deflate our goods, and egos. And then, if we were exceedingly fortunate, they would thrust one of those quick-fire multiple-choice questionnaires into our flour-covered hands; you know, those ones designed by morons for morons.

Question A
Aubergine is?
A a fruit
B a vegetable
C a type of Eastern European motor vehicle
D a tavern in France

Question B
Brioche is?
A cake
B a railway station in Paris
C a cookery method
D bread

Question C
The term 'au bain-marie' literally means?
A my beautiful mother
B goodbye for now
C to cook gently over hot water
D what do you mean, you cocksucker?

Question D
Hard-boiled eggs are cooked for?
A six minutes
B three minutes
C three hours
D three days

Christ knows what they were doing to eggs at some of those joints! No, no, my mind was reeling and the thought of staggering back to another hellish night on the grill kept making me spend another ten minutes in the Fattened Dachshund before I started that trudge to my destiny. If only my old man hadn't countersigned those goddamned forms. Still, until something better came along – like being the getaway driver on an airport job – I had to bide my time, that's what I'd do, line up some kind of opportunity and then blow this gig and let these crazy fools argue among themselves whether a fucking squash is a fruit or a vegetable.

At least during college Billy and me got weekends off, and by that time we weren't in any mood to negotiate that arrangement. More often than not Billy would catch the mail train up to his homeland and I'd hang around the Flatulent Dachshund or sometimes even go home myself to the hood just to be free of that ball-breaking and spirit-crushing hotel for forty-eight hours.

If Billy didn't have the money to go home, which he regularly didn't, on occasion he'd accompany me. The first time I took him, after we'd been at my house for a short while my mum took me aside and said, Darling, we know you like to help vagrants, but must you bring them home?

Vagrants? That's Billy! I told her.

Good Lord, she said, how did a man that old get an apprenticeship?

I had to explain that Billy just looked old, but even after that she still thought he was middle-aged, maybe it was the slippers?

On one late-night journey home alone, I met up by chance with an old school friend – and for sure we had been pretty thick during a certain time. Anyhow, this schoolyard pal of mine and I shared an otherwise deserted rail carriage toward our hometown and as it rattled along past new housing estates he filled me in on how his life was going. And to be sure it wasn't going anywhere fast.

Of course I ought to have known that he'd become a banker – especially after the sly bastard had diddled me on dinner tickets time and again – but somehow sitting there half-cut being lulled by the train's lullaby I couldn't help but feel pity for the poor fool. Okay, so he had a secure job, regular hours, a chance of promotion and a financial portfolio, but Lord God himself only knew how mundanely regulated that guy's life was going to turn out. I could see it all: house on nondescript estate, plump wife with pretentious ambitions in interior decorating, lawn to manicure, kids to groom, dog to bath, trash to take out, bills to pay . . . ye gods, my head spun, maybe I had made the right choice after all?

As we parted on a desolate and rain-buffeted platform he commented sardonically on my dishevelled appearance and junkie-like eyes. Are safety pins de rigueur in the cheffing world? Indeed they are, my friend, I told him – and by the way, are any of the pubs still open, do you think? The last time I ever saw him he was disappearing fast into the thickening fog, briefcase swinging and umbrella tapping the ground madly like Blind Pew himself, eager to deliver another black spot and ruin some poor bastard's credit rating for life.

11.

We're All Crazee Now

They gave us a break from college. Back at work in the hotel kitchen and there was too much silence for my liking.

When the kitchen is *too* quiet you get the creeps – because big kitchens are never really still. You know for sure that either someone has died or one of your colleagues is deep in the proverbial craphouse. But why were all of these hopheads staring at me? I couldn't recall whether I'd transgressed some rule or other, written or unwritten, although I was pretty certain that I hadn't. Next Billy arrived and everyone started staring at him instead. Just what the bloody hell was wrong with everyone? And then the Duce rolled up, attired in his tweed two-piece, and ducked straight into his office without so much as a bye or leave you. No one really wanted to tell me anything about it.

What fucking 'it'?

I persevered to no avail. I ran the loop, fuzzy as it was. Nothing stuck out as too OTT or against the house rules. I'd even stayed back voluntarily last Friday night to learn a little more about the basics of butchery.

Eventually, the Duce reappeared from his office, bedecked as usual in the cleanest set of whites in the joint. He had a quick head-to-head with a few section chefs and I watched the eyes of those watching the Duce and grew alarmed when all of those eyes were suddenly peering in my direction.

The Duce was upon me in a flash, but not in any savage vulture-like way; he was interested in my thoughts on today's menu choices. What kind of brutal savagery was this? As if I was going to contest the choice of one potage for another.

Something was afoot and whatever it was, it wasn't going to be coming direct from the *Good News Bible*. Next I watched as the Duce spoke with Billy in a fatherly way, and then I noticed three or four F&B types hurry past the stock urns and vanish into the Duce's labyrinth.

I shrugged as I caught Billy's nervous glance in my direction. Whatever shit was about to start its slide downhill it sure looked as if Billy and me were right in its path. Finally we were summoned to the den, and from there escorted by the posse of F&B men up the back stairs to a disused office.

We all sat there edgily – Billy and me, management, the lawyers, and a medico – looking at each other until the Duce finally joined us. They all went about their business of shuffling through paperwork whilst striving to appear impartial – I was used to such conundrums, but not Billy, he was as jittery as a grass in lock-up.

Cool it, I whispered to him, but I didn't hold his hand.

My recollections of that meeting are hazy at best, although I remember the Duce telling me that if you want to fell a tree you start at the bottom? Maybe you do, maybe if you're a lumberjack you do. I didn't see the correlation; what the fuck did trees and old woodsmen's sayings like 'sometimes you can't see the wood for the trees' have to do with our delicate situation? Many years later, however, lying under the shade of a palm between shifts on a white beach in Somerset, Bermuda, idly dragging on a joint the size of a field gun, I finally got the point; to be sure, I wasn't then renowned as the great thinker that I am today.

It all had to do with paper – they make paper from trees and in the main they fell all of that forestry just to keep the mills of accountants humming along nicely. That was what it boiled down to, very fucking dodgy accounting. Bankruptcy, that was the bottom line, too much out and not enough in, as they say in the brothel game. And ever since that murky day, I have had nothing but the lowest contempt for anyone working in the financial sector.

These bean counters are like those South American suckerfish that enter a man's penis and devour his whole innards. How many times since that day have I heard that word has come down from the Tower to cut loose a few goons to save on the wage bill? Too many I guess, though never once have I heard of the bean counters sacrificing one of their own in the name of fiscal prudence. Anyhow, the upshot of our little visit to the backroom was that we learned the hotel was up shit creek without a canoe, let alone a fucking paddle – for reasons that did not need to be made known to first-year apprentices, though I got the gist anyway, that is my skill. Many people were trying to bail out the red ink the place was drowning in, and the time had come to attempt to salvage some kind of financial respectability. The first to go would be the last apprentices in, even though we were paid the lowest salary in the whole damned joint. To be sure, it must have made sense to someone to shave twenty-two quid a week off the wages bill instead of ditching a few overpaid management types overboard. The hotel was becoming some kind of flop house for the financially reckless.

What can we do? Billy asked while he sucked vigorously on his asthma inhaler.

Fuck-all, I said – which didn't appease his concerns.

That very afternoon, the Duce told us, we were to walk along the promenade for about a mile and attend an interview at our sister hotel, which was interested in picking up the slack, so to speak. In hindsight, I guess that was a better option than being thrown out on the street like non-paying guests, but at the time I'd rather have walked the damned plank. So with heavy hearts and furrowed brows we trudged up there and got sent to a new Duce's office by some spotty clerk. Told to sit and wait for the hour of execution. Already we had bad vibes, as they say in the markets, for unlike our rather homely kitchen, this place appeared to be staffed by one of those chained-together labour gangs you sometimes see along the highways of Alabama.

The place gave me the creeps, from its leery chefs to its evil-looking KPs, from the abrupt porters to the surly front-of-house chicks. I didn't like it, not one bit – but it was either this, or take a hike.

I do not know if you recall the film *Midnight Express*, but if you do, if indeed you've ever tinkered with the idea of smuggling hashish out of Istanbul, then you will recall the evil warder of the Turkish jail our hero was thrown into. Well, if you attire that guy in chef's whites, add a pair of large specs, top it off with a three-foot hat, then you will have some idea of what our new Duce was like. Indeed, he was a skulking brute of a beast, the kind of man who you could safely assume, even on first impressions, would be happy to acquire a couple of new grunts to skin. The kitchen hung heavy with a sullen kind of fear.

The kitchen brigade huddled over stations brooding like hens on the roost. The overall intelligence quotient appeared to be around the range of an incestuously bred stoat.

And this was to be our new home, just as soon as we signed the papers to transfer our bodies. No legal representation was offered, and we sure didn't know how to ask. We would be here in a week, treading water in this vast expanse of heat and indignation like a couple of survivors from the USS *Indianapolis*.

It was, as you can imagine, with surly resignation that we traipsed back to our old hotel. Jesus H. Christ, you get more time to ponder matters on death row than you do in the cut-throat world of the big hotel.

Nothing ever stays the same, not in cheffing and not in life. I had learned this much if I had learned any damned thing, but the thought of sliding down another snake and being back at go really did irk me. As for Billy, well, by that time he had just about had a gutful of professional cookery and the misery it entails. He wasn't even certain he would make the move; maybe he'd just head home and look for something in the aged-care sector.

C'mon! I geed him up. We can take on those cretins!

He wasn't sure though, Billy never was, and during that last week he was so shaky he couldn't even get a Bacardi and Coke to his mouth without spilling it.

Will and Ben had many a word of reassurance to plant in our mushy minds. They knew Big Daddy Steve-O and his goon-like offsider. They told us spine-curdling tales until we didn't want to hear any more.

Stripped of its prestigious star rating, along with most of its liquid assets, our old hotel slid slowly into the black depths of budget weekend breaks, never to re-surface. Sometimes, Billy and me would saunter up there, stand outside, staring up at our old room wistfully while the 2-star sign swung lazily in a limp breeze. Something good had ended, and something bad had taken its place – that is the way of things in the industrialized world; although not in the Punjab, there they have a far more fitting remedy to deal with rogue accountants – they run the bastards buck-naked through the streets while those who have been financially flayed beat them with long bamboo canes.

12.

Bohemian Rhapsody

It's time. That's what they say when all your stays of execution have been exhausted.

There is always gallows humour in a kitchen, but as I packed my belongings ready for the big move, I could find nothing to laugh about. Billy, of course, was even less enthusiastic about the sudden shift in the status quo. Don't worry, I told him, all we've got to do is tough it out and not let those bastards think we're weak at the knees or shit our own beds.

It was a surreal kind of feeling, for that place had become our home, and the members of that brigade our extended family. A kitchen nurtures you, becomes your mother, imbues you with a heady, swooning feeling of invincibility. It felt like Billy and me were off to foster care. Will and Ben offered to drive us up there but we graciously declined. Last time they had driven us someplace, we had endured a fifteen-mile walk back to town.

Instead, we hiked along the front like a couple of rent-boys new to town.

At the new joint, instead of using the tradesman's entrance as is customary, we steeled ourselves and walked straight past the bewildered doorman. Before he could shout, Hey you two fuckheads where do you think you're going? we were at The

Desk, where a flustered woman gave us a cold stare, the kind of once-over women reserve for specimens who do not measure up to their stringent values in respect of maleness. She pressed a buzzer and after a short while an F&B type came out with a piece of cucumber stuck on his chin. Ah! he exclaimed as if he himself had unlocked the code to life, you must be the two . . . chef thingies.

Ye fucking gods, what kind of a gin palace were these people running?

The guy looked as if he'd been recently sculpted from limestone and I couldn't quite pin down his ancestry. Well then chaps, tally-ho! he said gaily, and we followed him through a winding maze of back-of-house tunnels where periodically we had to stop to squeeze past overweight waiters hauling armloads of linen, and a few lumbering chambermaids carting around the result of an unwise decision. It was the other joint, but it smelled the same and it looked the same. When you have been deep in the bowels of one big hotel, you have been in the bowels of them all.

At the top of the stairs we re-emerged on a landing that had seen grander times, if the threadbare floor coverings were anything to go by – and then there was the telltale reek, the pong that emanates from live-in staff quarters the world over. I guess if you, dear reader, have lived-in, you will know immediately to what I am referring, but for those of you who haven't partaken of the privilege please permit me to fill you in. Hotel staff quarters smell like the clap: wafting odours of old socks, half-drunk ale, rotting food, cheap aftershave and soiled bed linen attack your senses, make your toes curl and your short and curlies unfurl.

Onward we trekked, hugging close to our lively welcoming committee of one, until we reached a small hatch at the end of a corridor that was strewn with the detritus of the live-in dickwad. A sock here, a shirt on a radiator there, some dried blood on the wall there, half-heartedly scrubbed vomit on what remained of the carpet, a few beer bottles, a bit of public lavatory graffiti and, near what loomed large as our final destination, a pair of size-thirteen shoes with fungi sprouting from them. It was charming in a bohemian sort of way, but it was overpowering too – just what kind of psychopaths resided behind those closed doors?

And then we found out. Just as the F&B went to unlock the door to our new cell, the door opposite opened and a cloud of ganja smoke poured into the hallway making the place look like Beijing on a good day. A fuzzy-headed Afro type was standing there scratching his nuts, a half-burned reefer the size of a blunderbuss in one hand and a can of something in the other. The dulcet tones of Mr Marley drifted through the haze and the F&B suddenly had a look of panic on his face. Well, here it is chaps ... it's not much I know, but we're re-doing some of the rooms upstairs and hopefully we'll have you all shipshape and Bristol fashion before you can say crackerjack. And with that he morphed into the cloud like one of the Wright brothers.

Meanwhile, the mostly naked Caribbean brother was hanging on his doorframe like a string of beads in a brothel. Him always says dat, man, he crooned, then took another deep drag on his joint and started laughing to himself rather crazily. It was only mid afternoon and the guy was about as high as a migratory swift that had just caught a thermal.

As we stepped hesitantly into the cell, my mind was flooded by vivid memories of other times. The bunk bed layout reminded me of old friends and nights when you had to sleep with your arse hard to the wall. The view was magnificent in its nothingness, solid brick, the window jammed halfway-up; and when you leaned out a little, you could see you were peering down some kind of shaft, at the bottom of which lay a mound of garbage with furry creatures rummaging around on it.

Those are fooking rats, Billy told me matter of factly. And those buggers can climb too. Well maybe so, if anyone ought to know then it was Billy, he had grown up on a rat-tip.

And what the fook's this? he continued, holding up a bottle with a candle in it. It was one of those Matty Rose bottles that were all the rage back in '76.

That's de light, man, a mellow voice said, and our Rasta friend loomed large in the doorway like a mugger in Kingston Town. His name was Errol and he was Birmingham born and bred. He offered us a toke, but we declined his gracious offer.

Where's the shithouse? Billy asked, and the query sent our new friend into spasms of raucous laughter.

De shithouse! Man, you boys ain't livin' in da fuckin' Ritz now! Only one shitter, man, and him's always backed right up, get yourselves a bucket eh!

What kind of a dump is this place? Billy asked, and Errol just rolled his eyes and shrugged his shoulders. Dis is paradise, man, ya dig?

It was a bad scene, to be sure. Every miscreant, waster and nut job from the four corners of the Union had apparently been drawn to this place like metal to a lodestone. Sometime later we ventured warily down to the kitchen, led by the unctuous smell that seeps from a large industrial kitchen the way carbon monoxide seeps from a coalface. We joined the end of the queue, and it had been a very long time since we'd been forced to stand on this side of the hotplates.

This was our first look at the new cadre we were soon to join, and by god they were a feeble-minded and slovenly crew.

We shuffled along the gruel line indignantly, being served the usual lukewarm muck. I had already surmised from appearances which of those clowns I could take out, should the need suddenly arise. This is one good aspect of having been incarcerated, it teaches you how to spot the weakest link. We moved along to collect our cutlery from the trays where a dwarf was balanced precariously on a milk-crate polishing the very same.

And don't cha be thinking you'll be grabbing yerself some of me nice clean stuff ya fecken heathens – up there's yer tools, he growled maliciously. Billy gave me a raised eyebrow and we both moved along to get some tarnished forks.

A fucking leprechaun too, now that's gotta be bad fucking luck, he offered disconsolately. Whether the guy was a leprechaun or not one thing was for certain – there wasn't any pot of gold at the end of this mud-coloured rainbow.

Later we spent a tremulous evening listening to the rats climbing the walls, while the almost burned-out candle flickered gamely against a breeze that wafted in from above.

Christ I need a fooking shit, Billy moaned. He always needed one; Billy was a regular kind of guy.

Do it out the window, I advised him.

And get me arse bit off by fooking rats? Guess I'll have to brave the shitter, if I ain't back in an hour, call a priest.

Waking up in a strange place on the first day is the worst feeling of all, but at least we were still together. Okay, I was together, but you know what I mean. It would be upon my shoulders that the onus fell, I would lead and Billy would play second fiddle. We dressed slowly. Billy still didn't have clean gear . . .

Where's your hat? I asked him angrily.

I lost it at college, I think.

You can't go down without a hat, that crew'll eat you for breakfast, here, borrow one of mine.

I need a shit, Billy said, clutching his guts.

Another one? You've been shittin' all night, did you find bog paper?

Only an old newspaper, I've been working me way through the classifieds.

Christ, Billy, no hat and shit knows what state your daks are in, how in the hell are you gonna make it through till break?

Billy just shrugged and we set off, down into the hot steaming bowels. Whatever fate awaited us would pretty soon make itself known. In the staff lift we were joined by two chambermaids, the usual variety. Not even fanny could perk Billy up, though, and as we neared damnation he let slip the mother of all farts.

Oops, sorry.

One of the girls slid the cage door open quickly, and then she turned to Billy and called him a sick bastard. It wasn't the most auspicious of beginnings . . .

13.

Walk The Line

So, you're the shit-hot dickwad from up the road, huh? some unshaven waster masquerading as a professional chef said to me. Me and Billy had 'arrived' as they say on the train lines. Billy had been whipped down to the veg by some dopehead pedophile with bright-red eyes and rat-yellow incisors. Not me, though, for me they had Plans – knock the stuffing out of him on the first day, waste not a minute, men, on this scurvy dog. Shite like that.

I hadn't realized I was shit-hot, so their insinuation came as a surprise. But whatever, I felt able to handle a bunch of morons such as these with relative ease – except that mongrel of a sous chef standing over by The Book, that creep looked as if he'd feel not the slightest twang of remorse if he had to gut me along with the trout.

The goon who was verbally assailing me carried on his witless discourse, something about putting me on The Line.

Jesus fucking H., did he say the line? The line in a strange kitchen with leery gooks and a whole system you don't know on your very first morning?

Hell yes, that's exactly what this deadhead was talking about – the goddamned line.

Are you fucking sure? I asked him.

You can cook, bitch, can't you? the goon replied.

In a big kitchen the line is where you aim to be. Anywhere else is not respected. Filling chocolate éclairs with cream or fiddling about with fancy afternoon-tea trolley cakes while a group of your red-necked peers are going at it hammer and tongs over steaming bains just doesn't cut you any slack. To earn respect in a big kitchen, you walk the walk, talking the talk ain't nowhere near good enough – but hell, right here right now?

That's right, prickface, get your fucking apron on, another spook grinned. For a minute, I couldn't even remember what an apron was.

Here, the spook said, I'll be fucking mummy and you be a good little bitch, okay?

I couldn't breathe. I felt hot, my mouth was parched and my hands started shaking uncontrollably – and then the goon thrust the day's prep list into those very same hands and I wished I was back safe in the remand centre.

At the allotted time, the time when you have to move, your finely honed co-ordination of physical movement and mental astuteness combine with a pint of flat bitter and a copious amount of adrenaline to send your mind and body into a state that no committed drug addict could ever achieve. Those on the line who have indulged too much the night before, and baby that's most all of them in this joint, will be popping a little something to give them The Edge – whatever lifts your skirt works, okay? – while those who didn't spend the previous night rat-faced on the tiles are running on an endless reservoir of nervous energy. Service in a professional kitchen moves fast and furiously. Sizzling food is lined up on silver platters, spitting angrily on hot plates, and everywhere there is noise and an endless blur of hyperactivity. As the dishes line up, the pressure shifts from the chefs to the waiters, those idle specimens who have spent all morning placing bets for each other at the local bookies shop.

Once that swing of the pendulum takes place, you know you are in total control – and instead of slowing up, inexplicably you work even faster. It's a sick kind of pleasure that you derive from watching waiters crack under the strain. Undoubtedly it's a love-hate relationship and the more you hate waiters the further you'll go in the kitchen! Make the silvers red-hot, so that even a waiter with a sheaf of serving cloths won't make it to the dining room without losing his thumbprint, and you'll be a star. For no waiter in his right mind will let go; he doesn't want to give the smirking chefs the satisfaction, and he fears a hostile barrage of abuse from them should he have to re-order. 'New order' and 're-order', these are words no chef wants to hear, especially the latter. No matter how entertaining it is to watch waiters squirm, it certainly isn't fun to have to re-do a dish you've already done, and in double-quick.

Service is a game that only the bravest and the most cunning dare play – you don't find mincing pastry chefs or cold-larder goons on the line. But sometimes, like today, you do find dickhead apprentices, new kids on the block, with more huff than puff.

Right now, I'm looking at Mel, a quarterback sous chef with nerves of steel and veins heavily laced with amphetamines or someone else's prescribed medicine, and asking him about some item of prep.

What? he growls.

This, I tell him. What the fuck's this?

You have been in a kitchen before, dogbreath, haven't you? And by kitchen, I don't mean that canteen you worked in down the road.

Next he'll insult my mother I suppose . . .

Did your mother keep the afterbirth and chuck the baby out?

I think she did, I tell him.

I'm taking the mother of all risks right now, taunting this brute in front of his crew rabid to see me beaten to the filthy floor like a mongrel. He's thinking about it, and I stand my ground . . . though I can feel wet farts staining my underwear.

The clock is ticking, like his brain – and instead of hitting me, he just smiles. It's a cockeyed smile, a smile not even a mother could love, but it's better than instant pain.

I like you, he says at last.

Yeah, well don't be liking me too much, I'm not the settling down type okay?

When your turn comes to be on the line as an apprentice, to be one of those chosen to serve, you only get the one shot. Lose your bottle or cock it up and you're over to the pastry section before anyone can shriek 'new order!'. Jump in the cage and have a go and you join an elitist group, the crème de la crème of the hotel brigade – the front-line combat troops. These guys are straight out of *Apocalypse Now*: sous chefs and sauciers with bandannas and T's instead of toques and jackets, fish chefs with glazed acid-head expressions and Californian surfer-boy looks, veggie chefs too stewed to know if its lunch or dinner service, and a platoon of apprentices keen to sign up for that kind of twice-daily gig. And this brigade is marshalled by a second-in-command with eyes like a dead turbot. Much like this guy I'm telling you about, in fact.

On the line, you get to scream and yell, to release all that bottled-up frustration and tension. You get to shriek like some gibbering idiot just off his meds, and drink as much as you can handle without rebuke. You yell obscenities like Johnny fucking Rotten, sweat so much that you drop a pant size each day. You change into a person your own mother will no longer recognize as either human or family. At the bus depot when your mother does eventually see you again after long months, she'll walk straight past, shooting you that disdainful sideways glance she always gives to down and outs.

This was where I was then: looking at my shot, while a scabies-riddled crew of cut-throat mercenaries gave me the evil eye.

What goddamned time does the beer get here? I asked the nearest dupe, some rube with a scar right down the side of his face, and all the time wondering how he came by that mother. The rube just looked at me, kinda sideways, then carried on smashing garlic with real gusto. Oh mother, the shit bogs I find myself in.

How I got through that fucking service, I know not. By the middle of it I was pretty much tanked-up on other goons' slops, my mouth was running in fifth and the power steering was on. I found the right notes, the beat, the ginga, if you will.

It was over anyhow, somehow, and I was as shagged as a new-to-town cowboy trying to earn his spurs. I was sure that after this debacle I'd be down the pots for a month, maybe two – but instead the sous came up to me and, instead of grabbing my nuts, told me that my lover was a real fishwife.

What fucking lover? I spat ferociously.

Your wife over there, the bitch tit-deep in cauli. He was talking about Billy, of course, and he was affording me the opportunity to trim some fat so to speak, to dump some excess baggage if you will, join a happy swinging crew and leave Billy's flabby white butt hanging out there in the fresh new breeze.

It was sure tempting, but I am not the kind of person to

jettison my allies in their time of crisis, so I just laughed at him and swaggered off to get a fresh pint. That hophead would have to take us on as a pair – if he had the guts for it, which right about then I seriously doubted.

Finally, me and Billy were released for three hours. We had survived our first day in hell, but as we lurched tiredly up to our hobbit-like garret on the west wing, we exchanged just a few simple words of enthusiastic comradeship. Time would tell, it always does in big kitchens, maybe in life too. I was growing up too fast, that was for sure; if me and Billy were going to gate-crash this team, I was the one who could get us inside. I loathed the responsibility. By nature I'm a loner, but Billy was obviously past breaking point.

It's nearly fooking Christmas, he said to me disconsolately. I hadn't even realized; it's far too easy to lose track of such things inside of the whale. I hadn't even noticed the bags of chestnuts stacked everywhere in the kitchen, but Billy had, he'd spent the whole morning prepping them along with a hundredweight of cauli.

Christmas? I said.

I miss Christmas at home, don't you? he asked. And to be quite honest, I didn't. Christmas is just another day, and often one of the most tedious of the year . . . but not in the big kitchen.

14.

So Here We Are Merry Christmas

Christmas is supposed to be a merry season. A time of goodwill to all men, and women too I suppose, but not in the professional kitchen. Christmas month is like the *Texas Chainsaw Massacre* conducted on a turkey farm. Goodwill is in very short supply, but on the flipside, rum is plentiful.

In the kitchen everything is geared toward that one big lunch. The preparation is endless; day in and day out you are surrounded by nothing but turkey. Whatever happened to Christmas? I pondered as another pile of turkey legs got tipped on the floor right next to me for de-boning. Whatever happened to yuletide: to tinsel, wrapping paper, Christmas crackers, that funny chocolate money, goddamned presents? None of these treats held any relevance for me any more, for all I knew Christmas could have already gone. As the mountain of decapitated poultry bodies piled up, it began to look as if I'd never see anything but turkey ever again. Around me was frenetic activity; more deliveries, more new staff, more managers wearing silly hats, more of everything apart from bonhomie. Our job was to serve, and The Book had been damned right on that particular point.

In fleeting moments we chefs would gather at the nearest watering hole, a festooned hive of celebrating working types whose holiday was almost upon them. To have to witness this soul-destroying spectacle night in and night out, to sit there morose trying to coax the dregs out of an all but empty glass while the revelry of the normal world gathers momentum all around, is about as low a feeling as any person can achieve.

You know only too well that come the big day, these people will be gathered around a gaily decorated table buckling from the weight of seasonal delights. That after gorging themselves to puke-point they will continue guzzling alcoholic drinks until the time arrives to toast Her Majesty the Queen. Their day will be full of warmth and bi-partisan love for their fellow man, and his wife and daughters too if the opportunity arises.

At this time of year many of the chefs who have stood cheek by jowl with you through savage summer services will have fled to cozy front rooms where they can lie rat-faced all day until the pubs open again on Christmas afternoon or Boxing Day. And why the hell do they call it that? No one feels like pugilism the day after a belly-full of candy canes.

Into your swirling midst comes a squadron of casual types; people without families, obligations, National Insurance numbers or even legal work visas. People who throughout the year hide their lights under bushels while awaiting the opportunity to make quick cash working twenty-three hours a day prepping Brussels sprouts.

These vagrants foreshadow how you yourself might end up in a few years time; drifting inanely from big hotel to big hotel looking for any kind of low-rent gig to support your bad habits.

Sweet Jesus, I loathed Christmas. I still do, in fact.

Not all felt the same, though. Christmas to many in the brigade meant overtime, more dough, a genuine reason not to have to endure another extended lunch with the in-laws, and Hot Action. By Hot Action, I mean sex, of course. Yes indeed, for Christmas also brings to the big hotel a troupe of free and easy university kids looking to score big over the holidays, attracted by enticing notices sent to their deans and pinned up on their vacation-work boards, and by the whole crazy notion of being away from home at Christmas (assuming they actually have a home to go, that is). They come to us bright-eyed and largely bosomed around the week before the big day, and depart with saddle-bag eyes, varicose veins and pregnancy testing kits on New Year's Day. It is an adventure they will never forget, especially nine months later as they look into the eyes of their ill-timed offspring.

For the seasonally attuned members of the brigade, this is a time of plenty and easy hunting. Unless, that is, you happen to be an apprentice, in which case self-indulgence is a luxury you can ill afford. Your body, that worthless piece of meat that clings to brittle bones and covers already terminally damaged organs, is dragged from pillar to post by a posse of section chefs hell-bent on avoiding the craphouse cometh the big day. The Duce strolls around his manor carrying a blood-stained clipboard and a half-empty bottle of rum, one eye on the current stage of the meez, and the other on the nimble bodies of the new arrivals. There is much grist for his mill but, as the designated hombre in charge, the Duce must pay rigid attention to the finest detail, and indeed that is why his tepee is the largest of all.

Just when your brain switches to automatic pilot, you are seized by the Duce in a sleeper-hold and hauled dribbling from the turkey-kill pile to the vegetable section, where you are greeted by some smiling demented gook up to his nipples in carrots. This man is a new face, and to be sure he won't be fucking grinning for too much longer. The Duce is irate, shaking with fury, the reason being this damned fool has never even worked in a big kitchen before, in fact only yesterday he was stacking crates in the vegetable warehouse on the outskirts of town.

Suddenly eight apprentices and a dozen flea-bitten students are going at it insanely over two tons of carrots – the fool they hired couldn't even understand basic instructions. A bag, by Christ! the Duce bellows. Fifty bags, you damned imbecile! By week's end we are all afflicted with a severe bout of carotene, all a healthy shade of orange. And, as predicted, our new veg-meister is no longer smiling.

Sometimes in a quick lull you can take a peek into the pastry, where the geeks aren't even raising a sweat as they casually fill two thousand tartlet cases with mincemeat. But no sooner do you dare to stand still than you're nabbed by another section chef for yet more festive purgatory on some kind of food production line. A half dozen of you will be lined up at a bench peeling chestnuts for stuffing while idly chatting about Christmases past when you used to get up at five in the morning and . . . and then a section chef will overhear and tell you that Christmas Day in the kitchen is just the same; you'll be down by five in the morning or else they'll castrate you, you'll get a nice little present in the cold larder if there's time. And for the love of Christ you'll be the living dead by the time the Queen gets to speak, and if per chance you survive all of that, then just for post-lunch entertainment they'll chain you up outside and flog you with leeks.

Now stop fucking talking and get peeling.

These are the kinds of inducement they use to perk up your flagging morale.

The Duce and his henchmen will bust numerous blood vessels trying to keep the whole waterlogged ship afloat and your whimsical thoughts of all those Christmases snuggled up on the couch watching *Treasure Island* remain nothing more than someone else's memories that have somehow found their way into your stinking rotten brain.

Many people will crack under the strain of it all. First the larder chefs, their workloads having increased to such a size that even those with the most organized of systems will one day be found running around with a chopper screaming 'Destroy!' and 'Exterminate!' The Duce, however, is prepared for all eventualities; he has not risen to where he is in the world without having had to offload a few pillheads when the need arises. Rum arrives in the kitchen by the keg-load, for Christmas is no time to try getting by on bottles. Rum goes into every damned dish and pirate-like quantities go down the gullets of the brigade without even touching the sides. It is easy, once you have acquired a taste for the stuff, to comprehend how so many otherwise prudent travellers ended up in the cooking pots of cannibals. One too many rums can cause a man to start seeing the world around him with a vengeful mind and the hard stuff has a way of making many wandering minstrals dream of palm fronds, grass skirts and voodoo ceremonies on tropical paradises.

As Christmas Eve grows near, you hear a loud gasp of achievement from the brigade. The Duce holds one last inspection before he releases us from bondage on an overnight pass to debauchery and Satanism.

It's the night before the big one and the pubs are jammed with chefs loading up for the battle ahead. Carols are sung with merry voice as yet another overflowing tray of ale is plonked on the sodden tabletop by an unruly lass straight from a failed beautician's course. The boys continue sucking it back, and as fast as they suck it back the faster it's pissed straight out again in a urinal that has long since seen the deodorizing block vanish down the drain. People start free-loving everyone because it is Christmas. Complete strangers are suddenly overcome with the wild urge to shout the whole bar a round and lead a heart-warming rendition of Jingle fucking Bells.

By the time you are forcibly ejected from your Christmas Eve sinkhole even you have embraced the season as a true friend. Along the fairy-lit front many just-met couples are engaged in deep but un-meaningful relationships of the sexual kind and up on the hills of suburbia lights twinkle like a million tiny stars. Even the bums are full to bursting with glad tidings and for once their begging is being rewarded by the good folks who are full of whiskey and compassion for men worse off than they. To be sure it's a happy and lifting experience as a group of you saunter back to your home from home happily screaming God Rest Ye Merry Gentlemen at the very top of your collective voices.

And then the alarm sounds at five o'clock in the morning and you feel goddamned awful. Your head is pounding and your body aches – keelhauling would be preferable to having to climb into that bloody gear and take the express elevator down to Hades. Your roommate has soiled his bedding during the few hours that sleep has found you both, and the room reeks of stale urine, rancid chef's gear, tobacco and a half-eaten kebab. What at first you think is some kind of leftover curry turns out to be the vomit that your partner in crime has retched onto the floor about the time Santa was starting his biggest payday of the year. Jesus H. fucking Christ, you moan, as you hunt for clean underwear and a jacket that even half resembles the colour white. Finally your buddy is up and in the early hours of that Christmas Day he looks about a hundred and five; he reaches for a can of something that only a few hours ago a dozen or more chefs were using as an ashtray and chug-a-lugs the dregs in one, butts and all. After an ear-shattering belch the whole room smells like the front bar. Finally dressed, you both make for the staff elevator, where a queue of dishevelled and hung-over spooks are standing there looking like rum-sodden elves the morning after the present-wrapping gig. No one says Merry Christmas, for there is nothing even remotely merry about a scene like this. In front of you is the mother of all services and quite possibly your very last day on earth.

With these sombre thoughts at the forefront of painful heads, you arrive in the kitchen at a time when on Christmas mornings past you would have been rousting the oldies out of their slumber to get a crack at the pressies. This Christmas morn, however, you arrive into a world that is already ablaze with hyperactivity. The breakfast guy is wearing a Santa Claus hat and for some strange reason white wellington boots; he is mob-handed on the breakfast shift and is already as smashed as a wino on payday.

The Christmas morning breakfast is a short sharp affair, as many paying patrons wait instead on the very long lunch. Wellington and his minions are hard at the embellishments that so define Christmas Day in the big hotel – like rolling six hundred pieces of bacon and skewering them on cocktail sticks. There are still staff to feed by the busload, though, and two by two they trudge wearily along the hot plates while an army of grindstone-slinging goons slop yesterday's leftover scrambled eggs and bacon onto their plates.

The Duce is already in attendance dressed in his Sunday best, knee-deep in the freebies that have been dropped off for him over the past few days of madness.

Next the section chefs begin to drift in resembling bounty

hunters around a wanted poster, many having been conscious since eight the day before, running on nothing but tipples and adrenalin. They gather in the Duce's office like the KKK before a lynching and the Duce leads them in a reverent consistory. Sometime later they spread out in the main kitchen like rats infiltrating a ship's galley and one by one the apprentices are informed of what heinous fate awaits them.

Huge trays are going into red-hot ovens while turkeys are being pulled out of equally hot ovens and sliced with a precision that would make most skin-graft merchants proud. Everywhere is the smell of food: hot mince pies, Christmas pudding, stuffing, fucking sprouts by the pot-load, soups bubbling and gravies simmering. The work is all but done and now all we must do is wait for the first paying diner to enter the arena and cast his or her ballot. This lull before the tempest is a time for serious contemplation and indeed the Duce takes the opportunity to corral his troops and bestow upon them a small blessing; he has a silk draped over one arm and a *Repertoire* in one hand. As he speaks you can smell the cognac and cigars on his breath. He speaks solemnly and sincerely and he tells us all that this is going to be barnstorming fun and that when we have finished we will have earned our spurs. Keep your heads, he advises us, and do not panic, fear is the enemy today. At no time should we buckle even in the face of seemingly overwhelming adversity.

At eleven a small boy who looks like Oliver Twist comes around carrying a tray of glasses filled with rum. He is a member of the Lost Boys, of whom we shall talk later. This is our pre-service ration, a little snifter with which to wet the baby's head – for every service is like receiving a new child. Down the hatch it goes; the waiters start to hover around the hot plates, their eyes full of terror as the maître d' gives them some kind of benediction in Spanish. We are set, lined up like

Wyatt Earp and his pals under the fluorescents waiting for the clock to signal the start of ruination.

A few finger their tongs nervously, others sharpen their beloved blade one last time; is there anything that has been overlooked? Do we have enough rubbers, aspirin, plasters, water, alcohol, et cetera to get us through? This gig is straightforward. We will be serving five hundred meals; the first service will be one massive hit of three hundred covers split between the normal restaurant and the ballroom, which has been specially fitted out for the occasion with band 'n' all – there is no Richter scale to describe such a 'quake. After this we will face the relatively simple task of a second sitting of two hundred covers. Anything over and above that and we will be fucked.

Moments before the off, a few pastry types come around the line carrying small silver trays upon which handmade chocolates sit on decorative doilies. They wish us good luck and depart smirking – only later will we discover that those deadbeat sons of bitches had fed us laxative-laced rum truffles ... Who needs friends when you've got enemas?

We are given one final word to the wise: the ballroom service could deteriorate into a debacle on account of the waiting staff for that area being almost wholly made up of casuals. We should bear this in mind and be prepared for any eventuality. JAWOHL! we shriek at the Duce, or, as the fish section likes to shriek on such occasions: FUCKING A!

I am on the front line. The Duce feels as though I have enough of the right stuff – lip, he means – to cope with such an onslaught. Naturally it is an honour and I click my clogs together in appreciation of the Big Cheese's faith in me. My task is to adorn the plates full of sliced turkey with one slice of chestnut stuffing, two chipolatas and one bacon roll – minus the cocktail stick. It sounds like easy work, I know, but let me assure you that hot bacon fat and cocktail sticks fucking hurt. I had hoped to be on the gravy train, but that privileged position of dolloping on the jus has fallen to the Duce's favourite son – literally. Maybe next year.

The first docket arrives like a missive from hell. It's slow and casual at first, a steady well-spaced flow and many poor fools are lulled into a false sense of security. I am right alongside the aboyer, the big man on the verge of an aneurysm who's shrieking out the orders, and already I can feel partial deafness afflicting one ear. So fucking what? That's two weeks in the sick bay in the real world. Not only do I have to keep my eyes on the salamanders where tray after tray of rolled pieces of bacon and chipolatas are browning happily but I also have to remove logs of stuffing from their makeshift bains, cooking pans half-full of boiling water that are sitting inside the battery of ovens. On top of this I have to unwrap the stuffing logs as needed, slopping red-hot greaseproof paper all over the show and scalding myself innumerable times in the process; also I am expected to keep one eagle-eye out for docket misdemeanours vis-à-vis the ballroom service because at least nine-tenths of these casual waiting mercenaries have no respect for Das System.

Now you begin to see that what on paper appears like a task even a retarded chimp could undertake, is in fact a logistical nightmare. In this kind of chaos I cannot expect help from my colleagues; they will be far enough into the shit bog themselves to have any time to drag a fool like me back from the brink of oblivion. Both the Duce and The Book are relying on me – and as I grab that first log of chestnut stuffing I drip boiling water all over my feet where it runs into my clogs and scalds my toes.

We start off well, buoyed by false hope and a misplaced faith in our own abilities. For a hundred dockets or more we are on top and the waiting staff are taking one hell of a beating. We have our table orders up so fast that many waiters are facing a continual hell broth of verbal abuse and slurs about their manhood/sexuality/family pedigree/homeland et cetera. But then something quite unexpected occurs; from somewhere near where our good friend Mr Lim is larynx deep in overcooked Brussels sprouts, there comes a blood-curdling shriek, like a banshee in high heat.

What in the name of Allah was that? the section chef asks me, and I just shrug, having heard worst sounds outside league football grounds and inside the walls of HM's fine establishments. At first people think it is a bad and debilitating cut – but no, the shriek has come not from Mr Lim as first thought, but from a visiting pastry geek with lipstick on who is aghast to find that his pot of brandy sauce, which only an hour ago was sitting comfortably in the bain topped with a greaseproof paper round, has all but fucking gone!

What the fuck are those idiots doing down there? someone says.

And do you think hot-pink lipstick suits him? says another.

Poor old Mr Lim, he has mistaken the brandy sauce for the cheese sauce and has sent out one hundred portions of cauliflower covered with brandy sauce instead of cauliflower mornay. The pastry boys are in a state, a right fucking two and eight, skirts twirling everywhere like a fourth of July parade in Smallsville, USA, because now they have fuck-all to dribble over the already high-stacked mound of plum puddings awaiting special delivery.

The Duce goes berserk. He takes poor Mr Lim by his hired-for-the-day jacket collar and slings him away like an old rag doll into the waiting arms of two vicious-looking KPs who have been especially hired for such an eventuality. Next the

Duce grabs a bottle of brandy from the tray of a passing drinks waiter and lays the poor fool out cold just for the hell of it. There are two pots of cheese sauce sitting in the bain; I can see them from my spot on the line. The Duce empties the bottle of cognac into one of the cheese saucepots and yells for sugar. I lick my lips. Two pastry geeks arrive with an armful each of one-pound bags and the Duce empties about five into the pot. Problem solved! That is why he is paid the big bucks.

Service is beginning to go awry, however. I am out of bacon and short of stuffing logs but incredibly I appear to have enough chipolatas to feed fucking Hannibal and his army; ye fucking gods, have I inadvertently been putting two goddamned pieces of stuffing on plates and only one chipolata instead of vice versa?

Have you got more fucking stuffing? a section chef asks me breathlessly.

Not that I can see, I reply calmly, and this sends shivers and bad vibes along the whole of the line.

Fucking Mary, mother of God, we haven't even done the ballroom! the half-mad chef screams in despair. I try hard to think of a happy place but unfortunately none spring immediately into my rum-coddled mind. Today, the Duce had said before service, we would find out exactly what being a chef entailed – we would stand tall and be proud, and above all else we would not bite the hand that fed us; that was the code of the brotherhood. And now my brothers were running around like beheaded cockroaches. Some demented fool was gibbering on about there having to be fifty logs of stuffing someplace – there just had to be! I knew better, however. If I lost my head now and blubbered out a confession the Duce would be wearing my balls as epaulettes on New Year's Eve while he did the highland fling with the general manager's bit on the side.

I *was* finding out what it entailed to be a chef: subterfuge. Many animals had discovered over centuries that the only surefire way to avoid being eaten was to play dead; to be sure, it had worked in the human arena of conflict also. Just play fucking possum, Bruce had said to me once – whatever that fucking meant.

Immediately several runners are dispatched to neighbouring hotels to beg borrow or steal more stuffing; the Duce is a man of murky pedigree and he will not lose any sleep over having to steal should the need arise. The gravy boy is jerked from his prized position and dragged by the hair to the food bins over at the dishwashers – the Duce wants every fucking scrap of leftover stuffing brought back to me for a quick dunk in the bain and a whiz under the salamander. That ought to shore up our defences for a few vital minutes.

And then the Duce is there glowering over me like the Abominable Snowman. I peer up at his hat, which looks to me like a fifteen-tier wedding cake, and as my gaze drops like a free-falling parachutist I am looking into the mean, red, rum-blurred eyes of El Diablo himself. You haven't been giving out two slices of stuffing per plate, have you, you little cocksucker? he enquires menacingly, his big claws already in the strangulation position. My whole career is on the line, so to speak. If I admit to the Duce that I have indeed transgressed through my own stupid involvement in seasonal binge drinking my lot will be about as stable as a pyramid of champagne glasses in the hands of a shit-faced sommelier. I hold the Duce's flaming red eyes with my own, and answer him resolutely. I have been calling for stuffing for the past twenty minutes, but no fucker is responding.

RIGHT! the Duce screams. He is a blur of whiteness, a ravenous shark about to strike, eyes rolled back and jaws gaping.

The alcohol that my veins have already metabolized is having a soporific effect on me so instinctively I grab the nearest waitperson – figuratively speaking. Maybe around September she was a bright-eyed and bushy-tailed specimen full of hope for the Future. Right now, however, she is already well past the first stages of exhaustion. Life at uni is never this hard, well indeed, perhaps next festive season she will opt instead for the comfortable surrounds of her family home, or maybe a bar where the owners are blasé about religious celebrations.

Get me a half dozen rums, I instruct her, and as this girl hasn't the faintest idea about whom she should be taking orders from, immediately she is in an obedient frame of mind: anything not to have to serve those over-familiar cretins on table ninety-four and get my goods groped again, she mutters disconsolately.

And so what? Those people are paying patrons and they may grope what'er they desire – everything has a price in the big hotel, but alas, I have no time to fill her in on the point.

She thinks I am the head chef, and why the hell not?

No, stop, I tell her, fuck the six shots of rum, just bring a bottle and two glasses and be fucking quick about it – no, wait, make that two bottles and one glass, maybe just fuck the glass. C'mon, sugar, I bark at her as she pirouettes, not knowing if she is going or just on the cusp of coming. This is more like it, now I'm learning pretty fast about the custodial rights that big-time chefs enjoy. Almost simultaneously I have a tray of nibbled and dribbled-over stuffing pieces and a bottle of rum thrust into my hands from different directions. I am back in business, as they say in the trade. Meanwhile, downstairs, some flunky in the larder is rolling around the cold section like tumbleweed on the prairie while the Duce tears freezer doors straight from their hinges. It is an ugly scene, for sure, but I do not feel even the slightest twinge of remorse. Invigorated by the rum and the steadily growing heap of salvaged stuffing slices I can feel the tide beginning to turn my way. I have learned a valuable lesson, and that lesson is that there is no loyalty among legless swine.

We have been on shift for something like thirteen hours already. The kitchen has been cleaned until it shines like a brand new penny and the evening smorgasbord of leftover cold cuts and old vegetables have been cunningly disguised as salads. There are only the hardcore live-in types about the place now; those with families, mistresses and pressing obligations to dope dealers and bookies have long since departed to revel in what remains of the Day. For those still within the hotel day, however, it is a sombre period. We have no idea whether it is dusk or dawn and our senses have been pummelled to such a degree that not one of us has sufficient energy even to light a gas ring for our own grub.

Someone comes up from the larder holding a roll of chestnut stuffing as if it were the baby Jesus himself. This special yuletide log was secreted from all in the eventuality that the shit hit the ever-throbbing fans. Now, I know something of the existence of this particular log, that it had been made with a loving tenderness by a few of the boys and therein they had deposited the very seed of life itself. Whether this a true and certifiable fact I do not know, but knowing a little something about the filthy gang who are spreading the love of creation, so to speak, as well as the love for their fellow men, I for one will not be partaking of festive chow-downing.

This particular log, however, is for our good comrades still manning the pastry section, for theirs is a tedious long-winded gig that stretches well into the nocturnal hours; and after their day is done there must be food awaiting them.

I have one last chore before I depart the scene of my many indiscretions this day. In the confusion and the heat of battle it is understandable that some have been overlooked, so I make my way precariously down to the pot wash armed with eight turkey legs and six half-emptied bottles of rum. My down-and-out friends are, of course, buoyed by the fact that I alone have not forgotten the true meaning of Christmas. After this delivery I meet up with the gang to see what was going down and am advised that our good pal Helmut had arranged a winner-take-all pool contest down at the Randy Dachshund. I must come, naturally, because many side wagers have been made. Thus rather tired and somewhat off colour I nevertheless trudge down to the bar with the troops. After all, we are all survivors of the mother of all services and as such, we stand or fall together.

The evening is cold and at that time of the special day only the desperate are wandering the streets aimlessly, the desperate and apprentice chefs with cause to celebrate or indeed commiserate. Alas, I am not at my most proficient on the baize and as such the windfall is not as expected. Some time much later we drift back to the hotel finally hungry for food ourselves. It will not be fucking turkey and chestnut stuffing: good red meat and chips with mayonnaise is the order. As we eat, the half dozen or so of us who have fought this day and won, the magnitude of what we have endured in the name of earning a pittance begins to dawn on us.

To Chefs! says one cheery fellow, as he raises a glass full of something from the Duce's stock. A half dozen glasses clink in agreement. To Chefs!

Finally back in the same place I left eighteen hours ago I find myself unable to control a pressing urge to shit. There is a snaking line of stomach-clutching pale faces outside of the craphouse, however, and someone is saying that the bog-roll has run out . . . but there are plenty of paper hats if anyone is interested?

Yeah, I'll take a half dozen, I say.

15.

The Spiders From Mars

After the frantic exertions of the festive season, when the confetti, paper hats, streamers and uni girls have been discarded like so much trash, an eerie stillness descends upon the hotel as rapidly as a suicide jumper takes to reach the sidewalk from the eighth floor.

Many people are let go, and the Duce flies off to Rome to attend some kind of health-farm-cum-poker-tournament on the company tab. The over-friendly sous chef takes the reins, and let me tell you right now that idle son of a bitch is about as frequent a visitor to the kitchen during his period of rule as a health inspector. We apprentices are pretty much left to our own evil devices while struggling to navigate a captain-less *Bounty*.

The rosters have been drawn up a month in advance, and the Duce has left explicit instructions that the menus from the same time last year must be recycled; under no circumstances should any imbecile call for new supplies. There is a ton of shit to use up and when the Duce returns trimmer and tanned he will expect the coolrooms to be as empty as an apprentice's building society account.

And so be it, we loaf around between sections with nothing much to do other than reheat yesterday's soup and chop a bit of parsley.

Every fucker is on some kind of break: the Aussie fish chef has flown to Melbourne in the hope of picking up some dole, the pastry chefs are away basking in the glow of a chocolate conference in Zurich, and even the fish boys are off California dreaming.

Much like the first few weeks on Pitcairn Island, no one really knows who is in charge and many petty squabbles break out among the apprentices. Some are of the opinion they are better versed in aspects of big kitchen management than others. The days are shorter and the nights far longer, and idle hands very often get up to the Devil's work.

Management, of course, keep a very close eye on the comings and goings. They are edgy at this time of the year – no one, not even the longest serving F&B manager, is willing to predict what might happen if the shit hits the fan and some freakhead decides to lead a mutiny.

Some kitchen flunkies suggest we should utilize this period of tranquility to hunt ghosts or dig tunnels – I however am not of the temperament to become a spook hustler. Others insist we should immediately form some kind of League of Chefs and institute an initiation ceremony that involves the letting of blood and the sacrificing of either live chickens or virgins. Where do these potheads think we are going to find a virgin in a big hotel? The question sort of puts the mockers on the plan. Most of these wasters are the voodoo freaks from the backroom, otherwise faceless specimens known in the trade as the banquet brigade.

We regulars knew better than to be sucked into their kind of hare-brained hocus-pocus. Well, most of us did . . .

The backroom boys are just kitchen hands who have turned rotten and other scurvy-ridden tramps who for one reason or another are unable or unwilling to get a grip on the intricate machinations involved with professionalism. They run a service line up on the second floor kitchen that feeds the conference rooms – and for the love of Christ, I never even knew we had another kitchen.

Fuck those boys, the sous tells me, on one of the few occasions he is actually in attendance, those whackheads aren't real chefs.

Many of these zombie types aren't even being paid by the hotel and are just shacking up in the room of some fish chef who quit about six months ago. Most likely they collect his pay each week along with social security giros down at the labour exchange (and that's an odd thing to call it don't you think, seeing as how very little in the way of labour is exchanged there?) while between times, they dance around the top hog of the banqueting suites like cabaña boys around Papa Doc.

Most of us main kitchen apprentices stay away from the Lost Boys, due to the fact they have a bad reputation for certain pagan rites that ought long ago to have been outlawed – and most likely were. On odd occasions after one of these gypos has dropped off a bowl of runner beans or a tub of newly scrubbed potatoes left over from a Dulux paints convention, he will shoot you a sly wink and give you the type of smile that woodsmen in Louisiana give to podgy Caucasian day-trippers. Maybe he will invite you to a séance in room 101 or something equally bizarre, or perhaps tell you on the QT that there is a full moon on the wane or the sap is rising ... supernatural bollocks like that.

Who are these people and what right do they have to be skulking around the big kitchen offering innocents poteen? Who knows? Perhaps the Duce, but alas his filing system is always securely locked and even someone with my skills with a hairpin can't get it to budge. The Lost Boys always unnerved me, and, as you appreciate by now, I am not the kind who is unnerved easily. I have spent enough time around those privy to the whys and wherefores of the spirit world – my own brother, by way of example, who spent the best part of his troubled child-years constantly stalked by his doppelganger.

I ought to have known that young Billy would fall into the clutches of these deviants – and to be sure I was not wrong. Despite repeated warnings from better men than I, Billy got hooked up in the great poteen drinking contest, held one night when normal patrons and shagged apprentice chefs were all for their beds. Off he went, whistling some Romany tune that the boys had taught him during a rather unremarkable service a few days earlier, carrying his tin cup and his sprig of lucky heather. Little did I know, however, that when Billy went off to visit new planes and astral dimensions that night, he would return to us some considerable time later permanently altered for the worse.

I had an inkling that things were veering off kilter, especially when the third-year apprentice installed himself as the de facto chef de cuisine and took to adorning himself with jewellery made from bones he had scavenged from the ever-simmering fonds brun. These oddities aren't unusual, many chefs have an unsettling peccadillo for self-adornment, and the wearing of boiled and bleached shin of veal bones as toggles to secure neckties was quite common practice. But not the wearing of chicken-bone earrings.

The poultry bones, though, were not the worst of the madness that appeared to have taken hold. Some slack-jaws had begun replacing the buttons on their chef's jackets with crab claws and equally appalling stuff. There was alchemy brewing in a large cauldron over near the steamers. These were not the kind of activities either The Book or Peter Pan had in mind for impressionable types; and before we knew what was happening it had already happened – sometimes that is the way such matters pan out in the abyss.

Eventually, the blame would come to be placed fairly and squarely at the feet of the cocktail barman, and why not? Later would occur an event reminiscent of a cross between the inquisition and a kangaroo court where much blood-letting and acrimonious backstabbing would take place. These events happen only rarely in the big hotel, but when they do it is best to align yourself with those holding the power – and cocktail barmen are not those people.

It all began innocuously enough.

Like I said, Billy went off to his fate with a bad case of the moody blues. Meanwhile, I flipped through The Book for school would soon be upon us again. The night wore on like nights tend to do and finally around eleven thirty I began to drift off. All was tranquil until around four, when all hell broke loose right outside our door. As I returned begrudgingly to consciousness I grabbed the moleskin-handled butcher's knife I had liberated from college during a coffee break last term. Hotel doors are not renowned for their sturdiness. No sooner had I pulled on a pair of filthy pants than the telltale sound of cheap hinges bidding farewell to a poorly made door frame began to fill the room, like bonfire night in Bonn.

It was a ghastly affair. No way was I going back down to management with some tale about caved-in doors again – they'd had a gutful of my deceit. I yanked that fucker inwards and three amigos tumbled into my abode all locked together like octopuses during the ritual mating season. At first it was hard to distinguish one piece of anatomy from another, for, as many sailors will testify, there is nothing quite so hard to disentangle than a ménage a trois gone sour. It was only when I saw that one of the stooges bore an uncanny resemblance to my roommate that I really got mad. What kind of fucking goings on were these?

Suddenly the pile of writhing limbs became unglued and, fortunately, I hesitated momentarily before hacking off a piece of one of the intruders to demonstrate my annoyance. Yes indeed, one I recognized immediately now that his ugly mush was free from my buddy's bottom. It was a cocktail barman called Trevor, and if that recognition wouldn't suffice in court there were also the fucking cocktail cherries all over the show.

Help me! Billy cried, and it was like a squeal from a piglet that was being yanked from the teat.

Immediately I sprang into action, though the barman was more slippery than I had first imagined. The third interloper I did not recognize, but he had vivid tattoos travelling up his spinal column like lumbago. As he tried to make his dash for freedom I couldn't help but notice he was also wearing ladies' panties – ye gods, what kind of a fucking gig had Billy gotten himself involved with this time? The urge to pig-stick the deviant bastard was strong in my mind, and then Billy shrieked again like an old lady who had just had her pension book snatched.

Are you fucking insane? I yelled as his assailants fled barely attired for such an activity, running around the damned corridors of a luxury hotel dressed up like drag queens looking for an open mic.

I didn't think I'd make it, Billy sobbed. And for a minute I didn't think I would, either, although I have seen many sights of the kind, you get to witness these when you are vacationing involuntarily in a building with barred windows and doors with judas holes. The reality of the situation began to hit home; my partner in crime had suffered the closest of near misses after having fallen into the clutches of cross-dressing party monsters badly hung up on making him their good-time girl.

There are many situations I will tolerate, but kidnapping and cross-dressers with little sense for colour choice or style are not amongst them. Nor are deviant cocktail barmen on my party list since that filthy night.

But, after all was said and done, there was nobody to tell.

After I'd mulled this problem over for a few days, I found myself with a simmering contempt for Billy's almost-abductor. Eventually I realised I should tell the sous, because if there was one person who was likely to believe such a fantastic story, and not only believe it, but revel in the persecution and retribution that follows such incidents, then by Christ, it was our trigger-happy chief-in-waiting.

So I did, and the sous got so fucking angry that he punched a hole right through the dry-store wall. We'll get to the fucking bottom of this, he told me (and you know, there was something strangely coincidental about such a line).

Word spread, because such stories spread through a big hotel like lice at a kindergarten. Some people were all for grabbing the son of a bitch after work, tarring and feathering the dirty bastard up at the local park – or maybe tying him up and tossing him off the pier. Others took a more philosophical approach, but mostly they were potheads.

Billy started to receive a lot of motherly advice from the chambermaids vis-à-vis his brush with unsolicited penetration and spent a fair deal of time up on the girl's landing attempting to identify similar panties to the ones his attacker had been wearing, just in case such specifics were required by law. Others thought that Billy had encouraged the whole mess through his complete ignorance of homosexual protocol, but these people were quickly silenced by a hit-squad that had been thrown together. Still others wagered that the Lost Boys had played a pivotal role in the whole debacle, and most of us were inclined to agree with that particular school of thought.

One afternoon, the sous and his goons went on a purge of undesirables, like Ness and his henchmen, and by the time the bains were switched back on for evening service, a few drifters had had their heads busted and their shabby belongings run through the mincer. All that remained thereafter was how to deal with Mr Drink Spiker.

Much as many of us would have liked to do so, it is not feasible to abduct and mutilate a cocktail barman from his station in such a swanky hotel. There are some lines that even chefs can't cross and one of those is clearly marked 'bar staff only at all times'. When management gets a whiff that a chef is hanging around the house liquor it throws their otherwise impartial judgment into chaos. Many reach for the mace and others for the stun guns, for a chef on the prowl for free booze is not the kind of animal people want to see at the zoo. Some kind of street grab was discussed and then dismissed, for events that occur in the public domain almost always end up being discussed in open court by twelve folks good and true.

Finally the sous and a few heads hunkered around a beer-strewn table and had themselves a powwow. These injuns were the kind who took the part about an 'eye for eye' in the good book literally. All that we had to do was set a trap, one that involved some concocted cum-on played out by a cute-looking boy ready for the plucking. Fortunately, the sous knew of just such a boy. None of us bothered to ask why. Chefs have many contacts and it is often wise not to query the instincts or hang-outs of people high in the brotherhood. This boy's name, shall we say, was Pretty Boy, and he was a good friend of some of our brigade. Pretty Boy plied his trade among the many cocktail bars operated by big hotels, where at night the beautiful and not so beautiful people congregated. There are a hundred such places spread along the front like whorehouses on the Reeperbahn. They twinkle invitingly like a Kasbah ready to ensnare the gullible with their gaudy beckoning neon signs. Some are indeed cocktail bars for the well-groomed patron of the big hotel, whereas others are little more than illegal brothels. It is simply a case of knowing where to look, and chefs, as you will have gathered by now, are by nature and design creatures of the night.

There are kicks aplenty along the Strip, all tastes are catered for. This is Tranny Town, where the boys are girls and the girls are boys and where Mamma Nature has been shown the back door with an abrupt adieu. It was from this milieu of deviant types that Pretty Boy hailed. Once he had been a boy with designs on a career, until the neon beckoned him like a May bug. (There are worse ways to pass the time; accounting leaps immediately stage front like John Wayne Gacy at clown school.)

The kid was all for it, so long as the price was right – there is no code of honour amongst perverts apparently. The rule is simple: each man for himself.

With the deal conducted in a shadowy backroom, all was set for a week hence. The wheels, as we say in the trade, had been oiled. How the deal would pan out no one knew, so we worked and bided our time while the cocktail barmen became ever so smug. Chefs, however, are patient people, it is the nature of their game. Some people are born waiters and others are born chefs.

White Riot

To the untrained eye of the outsider, the big kitchen appears to be a hive of well-organized activity, but nothing could be further from the truth. Most days we are in the shit bog from go to woe. You turn up for work (if, that is, you even bother to turn up) ragged and dog-whipped to find that you have no section chef, or indeed you have one but he is not the kind of person who should be admitted to such an environment when a state-run institution would suffice. And often these are the least of the professional chef's worries: there are customers, managers and waiters to deal with in the course of another abnormal day. I tell you this in good faith, perhaps in a small way as mitigation for what I am about to tell you of the terrible and heinous deeds some chefs do to food to exact revenge or take out their frustrations; for professional chefs lead the most frustrating of lives.

Occasionally when I find myself in the normal more civilized world where people use cutlery and drink from glasses, and the word goes around that an ex-chef is in attendance, some wisearse will sidle up and shoot me a sly wink. More often than not said wisearse is simply a pervert and should be avoided. Some worldly wisearses, however, will want to know the Truth, exactly what happens to the food in that period of time from when it was happily munching grass in a meadow to when it ends up on their plate. People are interested in the nitty-gritty; they are diners and bon viveurs and they have rented chicks to impress. Usually I am happy to oblige and by the time I have spun them a tale or two, most of these jerks have taken on the pallor of a cadaver. For what chefs do with food is normally kept within the confines of the great walls – no one wants custom to slide off, so people are hired to convince you that this restaurant or that hotel has a reputation beyond reproach. My advice when you hear such dribble is immediately to cut up your credit card and consider taking a mail-order bride from one of those Latin American countries where the seeds are cheap and the alcohol percentage in the local booze will run a Japanese moped up even the steepest Andean slope.

There are many things that find their way into food in this kind of slipshod hovel: dead roaches, hair, fingernail chewings, bogeys, woodlice, rat crap or bait, Band Aids, old sutures and spittle to name but a few. Most of these ingredients the casual diner will never notice or indeed need to be wary of, for food stored and cooked at the correct temperature has about as much chance of causing harm as the Pentagon has of converting Iraq to Christianity. Say, for example, a chef with some kind of bronchial infection is forced to work. Said chef then proceeds to cough slimy phlegm all over the veal before it is bread-crumbed. Well, the diner need not fear, because as soon as that baby hits the deep fryer there ain't no bacteria alive that can survive (although the day might arrive when it can, and on that day the hospitality industry will be fucked).

In the industrial kitchen food is cooked at very high temperatures. An industrial steamer for instance, if opened incorrectly, will quite happily strip the skin from your arms and face before you can say 'Oh shit'. I recall one time when tins became quite en vogue in the large white metropolis and many chefs used to warm them before opening. Tins that are hot and bulging need to be pierced before they are run around the electric opener and if they aren't, then all you'll hear is BANG! And then several chefs and a dozen wait staff will be screaming in agony as they try to scrape hot ravioli from their skin and metal shards from their eyes. It only takes a second, you understand, just the merest lapse of concentration to decapitate a section chef and blind several waitresses.

The diners, however, need not be concerned about these types of incidents. They have sufficient on their own minds as it is, worrying subconsciously whether they'll be spending the next forty-eight hours talking to God or maybe bin Laden on the big white telephone. And of course it is possible that they may. Unwary diners enter a restaurant at their own peril, this is their choice, and no one is holding a gun to their head unless they happen to be in Laos, where restaurateurs take an altogether different approach to customer enticement.

No one thinks they are going to be poisoned, inadvertently or otherwise, and I can say with one hand on The Book that I have known only a few such incidents. The main problem appears to be shellfish. Personally I would shy away from the mussels, the clams and the oysters; food storage procedures in some joints are not all that they should be and shellfish have the knack of attracting bacteria in the same way that bad restaurants have of attracting slovenly staff. That is rule one, as an ex-chef I never dine in seafood restaurants because I prefer my intestinal tract exactly where it is and do not enjoy laughing at the toilet bowl at four in the morning, or indeed, any time. You might be different, but that is your lookout.

Fish is another area of concern. Good fresh fish is fine and dandy and only a complete incompetent could poison someone with a piece of fresh fish – but alas, despite what it claims on the boards, most fresh fish is actually freshly frozen in the Delta by bug-eyed spooks with no restroom facilities, and this is where the problem lies. I have pushed for many years to install a BYOF (Bring Your Own Fish) ethic but alas my pleas have fallen on deaf ears. Poorly trained chefs defrosting fish is a gut-churning sight to behold. Often they will defrost it in water, and sometimes that water, with the bloated defrosted fish floating in it like toxic waste, will still be under the bench a day or so later. Then there is the covering with cloth method, which is fine if the cloth is clean, but not so fine if it has been ripped from defrosting chicken pieces because the chef wants to catch last orders or watch *The Bold and the Beautiful*.

And then there's that ubiquitous cover-all, the fucking Fisherman's Basket. Oh yeah, the only fish that goes in those things is fish that ain't quite dead enough to keep still in the pig bin, and the basket refers to the basket cases who order it.

Chicken, of course, is a heinous beast and badly prepared chicken will reduce a grown man to a dribbling wreck within eight hours of digestion. Never eat roast chicken out, but if you must, avoid legs and thighs. That was the doctrine of most cannibals and it holds true today.

And now that I have single-handedly all but ruined the shellfish and poultry industries, I feel it prudent to move onto the cunning methodology chefs employ to exact retribution. On whom? you ponder. Well, on you, shithead.

If I am eating out, which, I might add I can rarely afford to do these days, and I am served a bad meal, say a side salad with a bright-blue sticking plaster in it or a steak that has not been cooked to my explicit instructions, then I may complain, depending on the surliness of the wait staff, but almost certainly

I will not request any alternative or replacement foodstuffs. I am not that stupid, even though I might look it to the casual observer. I will also never advise my waitperson that I am an ex-chef, a foodie, or of any other occupation past or present that is somehow tied to food. What kind of idiot thinks it is okay to tell the kitchen beforehand that they are savvy about 'good food'? Ye gods, you might just as well draw up a stool and rummage through the pig bin. I can tell you exactly what goes on when the docket arrives from such a 'patron' because the waiter knows to pass on these insidious communiqués.

Your order will be handed to the chef along with your message: so and so on table whatever is some kind of fucking gourmand and has asked me to tell you that he or she is . . .

Tell someone who fucking cares, the chef will immediately reply, and from there it is a slippery dip. Your docket will be passed from section to section like it carried the plague and almost every goon that gets his hands on it will spit in disgust. I mean Christ all fucking mighty, you don't go to the doctor and tell him you're up with the latest developments in vaccines do you? No indeed, you trust your doctor to be a person of professionalism and virtue, but just because you subscribe to *Gourmet Traveller* or *Vogue Living*, you feel that it is your god-given right to pass on advice or ask the dumbest of dumbass questions:

Waiter: The gentleman on table eight hundred would like to know whether the venison is local or imported.

Chef (opening box of imported frozen venison steaks from Cuba): Jesus H. fucking Christ, tell that meathead that only yesterday it was having a ruck in some glen in the Scottish highlands.

Waiter: The golfing ladies on table ten wish to know your recommendations.

Chef: Are they hot babes?

Waiter: (Shrugs)

Chef: Tell them I recommend Burger King.

You get the picture. No self-respecting chef up to his fucking chin in dockets has the time to indulge in these kind of limp-dicked questions. I mean who the hell are you trying to impress anyhow, asking where the fucking venison comes from?

Next, of course, there are those diners who insist on perusing the menu as if they were in a sleeper carriage on the night train to Coq au Vin, then decide to ask whether a dish can be cooked differently/amended somehow/prepared without such and such/be served bloodless. Who are these cretins, and why are they in my restaurant? If a dish says pink lamb cutlets served on pureed fava beans then why the fuck do you think that the chef would cremate your lamb cutlets and serve them on mashed potato? What kind of an imbecile are you? If you want to eat food like that then do so in the privacy of your own home, for god's sake. Rule two in the kitchen reads: the customer is never fucking right.

Then come the serial complainers. These fools will send back anything because they feel that by doing so they are demonstrating to their dining compatriots just how avant-garde they are vis-à-vis the fundamentals of professional cuisine. These people are known in the trade as whineheads, and their complaints are never treated with any degree of compassion. Usually their food is dropped straight on the floor and kicked around by a few apprentices before it is grabbed up and thrown in the deep fryer. Sometimes, nothing is done to the dish at all other than have a few goons finger it before it is returned. The very worst complaints you can make to the kitchen are that your meat was under or over cooked or that your spicy dish was hardly spicy at all. These kind of comments don't sit at all well with the chef and you can bet your last dollar that your replacement food will be virtually raw, cooked to a cinder, or liberally spiced with every damned ingredient the chef can find at hand including rat bait. It is most unwise to return food to the kitchen. Not only can it be bad for your health, but most chefs have very long and bitter memories.

And then inevitably we're plagued by the curse of the goddamned herbivores. Just why in the hell are these people coming to a restaurant anyhow? A kitchen is a killing field, bad fucking karma or not, that is our job and there is no place for sentimentality. We will kill and eat every damned thing that walks, crawls, swims or flies and then more besides. If it was legal like it is in New Guinea, we'd broil up humans too. These dining trends crop up periodically, and every once in a while a bunch of righteous freakheads will insist upon their right to inflict on everyone else their latest doctrine.

Nowadays, of course, hospitality has strived to distance itself from the steely-eyed views of chefs with a beef about herbivores, and more and more we find these types catered for with a range of tasteless and protein-less dishes that are fit for neither man nor beast. There is incredible profit to be yielded from a sack of lentils and a few handfuls of tofu and many bean counters have seized the opportunity to insist the kitchen reap handsome dividends from our rocket-nibbling friends.

The most savage treatment of food, though, is usually reserved for the hotel's staff and its management. Watching staff line up for its daily gruel is like watching a documentary on Biafra. If Bob Geldof saw the state of the average live-in hospitality worker in Britain he'd pretty soon be getting the boys back together for some kind of Hotel Aid gig. With a mix of grunts like this under one roof, the big hotel has devised many cunning ruses to fleece these sorry bastards financially, while simultaneously feeding them food that barely resembles any recommended form of nutritional intake. In the big kitchen it is the worst chore to find yourself on the staff chow line ladling up a water broth that looks as if it has vomit in it.

On the staff line everything arrives accompanied with chips. Vegetables, when they do turn up, have already seen at least three regular services and re-heatings. Most foodstuffs will have been pureed to disguise the colour, and almost all of the food served up to staff will have been located that very day by a few chefs eager to offload some rancid meat or mould-encrusted wet dish they have gleefully discovered in the far-flung recesses of the coldrooms. Here, they tell you, thrusting a container into your arms, tart this fucking lot up and get rid of the fucking stuff before it evolves into an alien life form. After you have de-moulded said item you will have to find a way to camouflage what it was in a previous incarnation. Normally this task is accomplished by fossicking around the various sections looking for old soups or sauces that can all be mixed together and affixed with some fancy-sounding label. To be sure, it is a vile-smelling and awful-tasting concoction that will be greeted by the grunts with much gnashing of teeth and whingeing. But, after all that pantomime, you will find the mob happily chowing down on their feed like hogs at a trough.

And here come the F&B gang, all dollied up in suits, with the flower of the season in their lapel. Waiting for these wasters to choose a meal from the main menu is like waiting for Quentin Crisp to decide on a shade of lipstick before going out. Naturally they will always be the last to eat, as theirs is a supremely busy life. You will receive a docket in the wee small hours and invariably it will entail unloading all of the prep trolleys from the walk-ins or turning on every goddamned appliance in the place just to rustle up one meal. When it comes to *their* food, management aren't too fussy over expenditure all of a sudden. After another long night on the ranges, the stay-back chefs have had more than they can stomach of such shenanigans. Steaks are yanked from the meat trays in anger and slung around like a baseball. Chops are used as basketballs with the bin-holes on the benches used as nets, vegetables are scavenged from the still to be emptied bins and, as these morons are afforded the lowest possible contempt, it isn't unusual to see a steak pass between several sets of bum cheeks before it hits the flattop.

Ye gods, some of these recollections make me squirm just thinking about them, for what kind of heathens were we?

Enough of this anyhow, no doubt by now you'll be reconsidering that dinner reservation you've got booked at the swish place, where they take your coat at the door and give you tasty little nibbles while the chefs . . . yeah.

Bon appétit.

17.

Children Of The Revolution

T-E-A-M & T-I-M-I-N-G. That's what professional cookery is all about. I might have given some of you the impression that a hotel kitchen is just a hotchpotch of psychopathic gangs, but come service time it's all about the TEAM. Okay, so during prep we can fool about and take the piss, grind a few axes and maybe even exchange a few blows, but come curtain-up we're congealed again like a blood clot, forced by the nature of the game to all pull together in the one direction, oarsmen under the lash of a tall white brute.

If the hors have gone too early or too late then the fish is fucked, if the fish is delayed that puts the onus onto the sauciers and the grill chefs, if the main comes up but the veg chef has lost it completely then it's useless sending up the mains. And that is just the sequence on the line.

If the larder buys a big one and the raw materials aren't coming over as fast as they've been requested then the service quickly disintegrates into a farce. Many people will lose their heads in such situations and quite a few might grab the nearest utensil and begin attacking any passing apprentice. Fish chefs are the worst, for theirs is an art that depends upon split-second timing and theatrical delivery – poissoniers are not the kind of people you want to force into the shit bog through your own stupidity. If you have ever had the misfortune to be smacked around the head with a Dover sole, you will know why.

On the fish section, the buzzword is 'syzygy', and although I never quite understood what it meant, it sounded pretty fucking snappy. Since acquiring a fish-section vocabulary I have enjoyed many heated debates around scrabble boards vis-à-vis the legality of such a word.

What kind of a fucking egghead are you? irate opponents will rage, I thought you said you were a fucking chef? Syzygy, my fucking bollocks.

Of course I am always pleased to be able to point out that in any reputable dictionary, the word refers to a perfect alignment of the earth, moon and sun. It is syzygy that is required in a professional kitchen twice a day, three hundred and sixty-five days a year – and that kind of cosmic karma is fucking hard to come by.

Some awareness of astrological influences is required in the psychological profile of the professional chef, but on some days even Nostradamus himself would have been hard fucking pressed to predict what iceberg lay ahead. That is the beauty of the Game.

It started off like any other service.

This mob were a crew of pig-dogs, each and every one venal in the most unsubtle of ways. Right at the very top stood the Duce, though to be sure it was obvious to even the most myopic disciple that the Big Cheese couldn't hold on much longer. Most days he stumbled around like a junkie in rehab, groping for the nearest solid structure to stabilize his unsteadiness. The man was a feeble effigy of what had once been a proficient ruler. And the sight of the great man muttering to himself in shadowy recesses didn't bode at all well for the futures of any of us.

One thing you won't die of in a professional kitchen is an overdose of time, but when age and alcoholism catch up with you, your gory days on the range are numbered. As for the Duce, well his menu craftsmanship wasn't all it could have been, not even on a par with what it had been only a year ago, they told me . . . and matters like these have a way of unsettling the whole brigade. This crew was jittery and management had begun to keep a watchful eye on the whole ungracious debacle.

As had been predicted over ale, the whole affair came to a volcanic eruption like a giant boil on an accountant's backside. The Duce lost it all during one bad mother of a service where for one reason or another the brigade had prepared an entirely different menu from the one customers were ordering from in the restaurant.

What the fuck is this? I said to some flunky from the wait staff.

He eyed me warily for I was new on the line and no one knows how volatile some new chef might prove to be. Eez docket, que? he finally replied, insinuating in his own pidgin English that perhaps I had never seen a real one before.

That maybe so, Pedro, I replied smugly, but it ain't a fucking docket from tonight's menu, eez it?

This is the kind of jingoism that professionals converse in, you understand, and I write it here not for scandal's sake but for authenticity.

The waitperson shrugged nonchalantly. I just take the fucking orders buddy, cooking's your problem, capiche? And that much was true, although on a night like this, I was already experiencing the labour pains of second thoughts.

What the fuck's holding you up scumface? a section chef enquired of me, which somewhat defused my ticking bomb.

This, I replied handing him the docket.

Jesus H. Christ, was all he said, and believe me it was enough.

In those days big hotels ran two menus. For the cheapskates there was the table d'hote, the set menu of the day that usually consisted of various leftovers, and the a la carte for the more cashed-up and savvy diner. The cheapskates always ate first: in they would stampede like a herd of wildebeest, and before you could even order a beer the whole joint would be rocking to the dulcet tones of ravenous heathens chomping on cheap lamb cuts. Set menu orders came thick and fast, like locusts.

It didn't take too much in the way of mental agility, however, to handle whatever part of the five o'clock swill you happened to be tending. People who eat cheap aren't too hot on things such as presentation, and a sprig of parsley most usually suffices. This is normally the cushiest part of the nightly feed, and everyone in the kitchen is in a happy mood – unless by chance there has been some almighty cock-up that no one is aware of until the fat lady begins to sing 'Arrivederci Roma'.

The section chef ran off with the docket as fast as a pickpocket at Mardis Gras. I stood there looking at the waitperson, who in turn stood there looking at me as if I were some kind of clink rigger. Now normally, as you are aware, I do not make it my business to disparage waitpersons per se, indeed a good waiter is as vital to the kitchen as speed – but regrettably there are not too many of this kind of waitperson to be found. Standards had already slipped in the wait industry, evidence of which was standing opposite me across the hot plates, and by that stage he had been joined by about fifteen of his colleagues who had formed an unruly and spiteful mob. This is the way of wait staff when they get the first whiff of ascendancy, a rarified, heady feeling.

The Duce was nowhere to be found. Every nook and cranny

had been scoured by an advance party of acne-riddled F&B types. In the restaurant the cheapskates had started to stamp their silver-plated cutlery on tables, while back in the kitchen a few goons had already lost it in a bad way. The pompous maître d' arrived on the scene, and from first impressions I could tell he was the kind of man who would have been more than willing to link arms with Uncle A and seize power by means of the jackboot.

The maître d' made a play for control; he grabbed all the dockets from his troops, and handed them to a confused spook standing nearby. I could see a look of frozen horror on that sorry bastard's face.

You cook now! the maître d' commanded anyone who was listening, of whom there were none. We were too busy arguing among ourselves.

What the fuck is going on here? I thought to myself, as all around me white-attired spooks ran about like wharf rats at midnight.

Next the sous turned up. It was his rostered day off but like all second-in-commands he had no life outside the nicotine-yellow walls. He was dressed in casual wear, good quality jeans and a Fred Perry T; he was wearing sunglasses because apparently he always did to disguise the effects of too many nights partaking of the company of Mr Brownstone.

Everything okay, fuckface? he asked some ashen-faced pothead after he'd grabbed him by the gooleys.

Then a more experienced F&B type finally materialized out of thin air, like he'd stepped through a portal. What appears to be the problem chaps? he enquired in a mellifluous tone. There are people waiting for their din-dins in the restaurant.

Ye gods, we had squandered a half hour already deliberating on the pros and cons of the scene rapidly unfolding like a poorly made napkin: when in hell would someone stand up on the plate and take a swing? The trouble was that screwing up during service in a hellfire kitchen isn't like running out of paper clips in the stationery department. No indeed, it is more akin to having jumped on the engines in full gear ready to quell a raging inferno only to find out no one thought to pack the hoses.

The fire just goes its merry way and it laughs and crackles right in your face.

What the hell have you people been doing all day? the sous screamed. This isn't the right goddamned menu! Don't tell me you cretins have spent all day prepping the wrong fucking menu! It was said to great effect and the ever-hovering F&B guy made a quick note in a black book. Most likely it read 'promotion' and was triple-scored.

Where the hell's Dick? the sous continued, and everyone shrugged aimlessly because no one had a fucking clue to whom or what he was referring.

Dick! he shrieked again. The chef, for Christ's sake! The penny dropped, like it does in those peek-a-view arcades along the front. The Duce had a name and that name was Dick.

Yeah, as in Dickhead, a chef along the line muttered venomously. Finally, out of desperation the sous whipped a dirty apron from under a bench; it had been slyly covering fish for several days and now everyone realized where that god-awful stench had come from.

This is the fucking halibut! he screamed again, like Jesus up on the mountain. I had not an iota of a clue as to what was happening, as I was too engrossed in watching the cutlery dwarf arm-wrestling some hirsute Mediterranean type over near the stillroom.

In the restaurant, of course, people were getting tetchy. By their own admittedly low standards they had paid good money to be fed and watered and they saw no logical reason as to why all they had received to date was yesterday's bread. More F&B types arrived; the kitchen began to swarm with suit and tie activity as termination notices were handed out. The back door had been wedged open, a foreboding sign of the merciless cull that was about to follow. It was like being in ancient Rome during those last acrimonious days.

Finally they discovered the Duce deep in the bowels sobbing on a pallet of laundry, an empty bottle of something hard beside him and the whole saga was well on its way to a farcical ending.

Well, that's fucking that, a nearby goon told me matter-of-factly.

Over by the Duce's office, the one with the 'For Rent' sign about to be hung on it, a gang-bang was occurring between the F&B, the maître d' and the sous. A peace was brokered; no one cared about the whys and wherefores right then, all that mattered was feeding the baying mob and getting service back on the tracks. Recycled menus were handed out to the diners, much to the chagrin of those who had set their hopes on retro roast beef followed by plum duff for dessert. A tedious service followed, full of backbiting and petty recrimination; management kept close observation as we toiled. During the clean-up there was much whispered talking – the big axe was about to fall and no one high up really gave a monkey's arse whether it took more than one swing. In the dynamics of the big hotel kitchen there are always those only too happy to play the role of the executioner.

During the next few days the kitchen became a seething hotbed of unfounded rumour. The Duce had gone berserk and hacked up two chambermaids, shit like that. It is not an upbeat day when you have to watch your leader led out the backdoor by security toward a vehicle with curtained windows. He was a proud man, they said in reverent tones as F&B rummaged through his office and began hauling out crates of gin and X-rated materials. The smell was in the air, heavy and repugnant – the unmistakable aroma of death. It was over within the hour.

One by one they brought us in for counselling. We had witnessed the fall of a once great leader, and it was their moral obligation to appease our concerns. Soon, a new Duce would be crowned and the kitchen would again be as fresh as spring potatoes. It was the beginning of a new era of prosperity – which was all bullshit, of course, but it sounded inspiring. Many people wagered vast sums on the sous being elevated to the pinnacle of the dung pile, while others felt he had shit in his own nest on that fateful night. Anyhow, by the time we returned from college there would be a new emperor perched on the throne like Solomon, and a new arse to suck.

The Duce was dead, figuratively speaking. Long live the Duce!

18.

Pinball Wizard

Good fortune had decreed that Billy and I should return to college forthwith and let the lower ranks of the kitchen hierarchy stab one another to death minus our involvement. And so we did, because in matters such as these, apprentice chefs enjoy no weight of opinion. It is a done deal, as they say in political circles.

Anyway, we were pleased to be the hell out of there. Providence had also smiled upon us in the sphere of financial dealings. As our new employers had not the least interest in carrying over our entitlements, nor in providing us with immediate holidays as recompense, our old place had been forced to approach the official receiver to pay us out the two weeks' leave we had accrued whilst in their charge. It is a fine and dandy feeling to be cashed up, no matter for how short a while – and chefs, I have found, have about as much respect for money as they do for the institution of chastity.

A chef loaded up with hard currency is a beast devoid of principles and unconcerned with such petty matters as long-term investment accounts and retirement funds. Chefs live service-to-service in the great white castle, where they have little need for money – this all changes, however, the moment daylight again falls upon their sallow faces and lab-rat eyes.

Most chefs can drink their entire week's pay-packet away in the nearest bar, and some, as I have already told you, don't even make it that far. Chefs are notorious for many things, and brazen and unrestrained borrowing is close to the top of the list. This is no doubt due to their dubious pedigree; for most it's a juvenile history of petty crime, police cautions and visits to decrepit magistrates, and they enjoy a huge advantage over those who've arrived straight from a life of privilege. No one likes a wiener or a crybaby; no one in a big kitchen has the time or inclination to mollycoddle some spoiled little brat who still wears super-hero pyjamas to bed. Those kids fall by the wayside. Sure some find enough spunk to make it onto the pastry roster or, even worse, on to one of those innocuous general catering programs, but more than a few head home for a life of nine to five in the local bank. What you're left with is the hard cases, the residual stock, kids too dumb and too mouthy to fully appreciate what kind of life they're setting themselves up for.

I have never known a chef who is not perennially in debt: behind on a bar tab, in hock to a bookie, on the brink of forced eviction for unpaid rent, or having again to pawn his few possessions to get that thug of a dope dealer off his back for a few days. This is the way professional chefs live and it would appear that they prefer it that way. Most, if not all members of a large brigade, have not the slightest comprehension of the value of money – to them it is a necessary evil, although in a large gangland set-up like a big kitchen, there is always someone from whom you can cadge.

It is never prudent, therefore, to let the brigade know that you are flush. Make this intrinsic error of judgment and you will pretty quickly find yourself handing over a wad of notes to a barkeep afraid that the slate is rapidly spiralling out of control. Chefs have few qualms when it comes to financial risk and exposure, and even less when the subject matter at hand is drinking away some other poor fool's windfall.

As you can appreciate, Billy and I had kept news of our coming-into-funds all very hush hush, and, in fact, had even taken to venturing further from the regular drinking haunts in an attempt to distance ourselves from the high probability that some grass would spread the hard word.

What chefs crave most, after alcohol and the occasional rut, is a set of wheels. A chef with a welded together junker is even more dangerous than a chef with money, because a mobile chef offers his co-henchmen the opportunity to spread their filthy seed and bad credit record further afield. Why shit in your own bed when you can shit in someone else's? So this was Billy's and my plan: take driving lessons and, with luck, acquire a full-licence with all its innumerable benefits.

There is little to gain but much to lose by allowing the pack to know your innermost plans or desires. Martin Bormann said almost the very same thing before he fled the bunker like a filthy brown rat carrying a bag of looted cash and sixteen bogus passports. All we had to do was make it down the line on payday with a poker player's face – no fucking singing, dancing or kissing slutty chambermaids, I told Billy sternly. No matter how much bread is stuffed in that envelope, you walk out of that office just as glum and down at heel as usual, okay?

Too fooking right, he said. But Jesus, I knew Billy too well, and once some freak got a whiff of Billy's bonanza, those jackals would strip him bare.

They do not pay chefs on a Friday. No pay clerk with even only half his senses functioning would commit such a suicidal act of hospitality treason. To give a chef a paycheck on a Friday afternoon would be like giving Attila the Hun the keys to Rome and a free drinks voucher to boot.

Pay a chef on Friday, and you might as well write off the largest and most profitable service of the week, that or start hiring in casual gunslingers at an hourly rate that makes most hotel accountants break down and sob. No hotel accountant wants to pick up that kind of tab when monies can be used for more pressing concerns, such as laundering.

Chefs, therefore, are paid on a more staid day of the week – like Wednesday say, because back then, Wednesday was half-day closing, and a paid-up chef had little chance of spending up big. You don't find hardcore chefs ensconced in booze holes on a Friday or Saturday night; on those nights they are deeply entrenched in the machinations of food service wars and all publicans worth their salt stake their financial success on the fact that chefs get paid midweek.

You grow acclimatized to such rituals, and Tuesday and Wednesday become the professional cookery version of the weekend. All runs smoothly, until you re-attend college and they begin to pay you on Friday afternoon and then for eight weeks you are thrust back into the seething and often confusing world of normality. Why? Well, because of Sunday of course, who the bloody hell wants a Sunday off? Okay, God, but apart from him? In England in the '70s, there was bugger all to do on a Sunday. It was a miserable worthless day fit only for picnicking families, devotees of DIY and religious types. There was no Sunday football in '76, no all-day liquor licensing hours, no fucking shops or off-licences open and never anything on at the fucking cinema. The buses and trains ran even less infrequently than during the week and for all intent and purposes if you were off on a Sunday and had not moved fast on

Friday night, you were stranded where you were, with no hope of a reprieve.

On payday I kept a straight face, deadpan, and walked in and signed for my pay. The old guy handed it to me with a smug smirk, and sister, that mother was bulging more than an IVF sperm bank. Jesus, I thought, I can't even get this fucker into my pocket, and as I struggled Billy passed me and also signed on the dotted line. That was when the fun really began.

FOOKING HOT SHIT! he yelled, and that shriek of delight drew the attention of every beady eye in the wages queue. I had two choices, leave Billy there to get rolled while I made my own getaway, or use my guile to extract Billy and me from what was going to be a very messy scene. Those hounds had smelled blood, though, and before I could get to Billy he was surrounded by wide boys and trashy chambermaids. He was everyone's best buddy and too stupid to realize that for him all was lost.

But not for me. I made haste to the stairwell – maybe those hawkers wouldn't realize I'd been paid out as well, they aren't that bright you know? I made it up one flight before I bumped into the concierge, who told me there was a hot rumour already in flight about me and Billy being flush. Fucking bollocks, I told him. As if a couple of apprentices are ever flush! It was a good bluff and it worked. So long as Billy didn't let on that I was in the money game too, all would be well.

And all credit to him – he didn't. His money, however, didn't even last two days; he was skint by mid-week as per usual and laying on his bed all forlorn and destitute.

You fucking idiot, I told him. Didn't I tell you to walk out of there stone cold calm?

I know, he told me morosely, but those bastards were all over me like mites on a sheep dog.

Well, if you're gonna shriek like a banshee, what do you expect, kiddo?

I was gonna go home too, maybe buy a new ferret.

A ferret? I thought we'd agreed to take driving lessons, how you gonna haul ferrets around without wheels?

On the bus. No one turns a blind eye up my way.

What, to a ferret nibbling your ear on the number 32?

Nah, stupid! You don't 'ave 'em on yer lap, ya stick 'em down yer pants where it's warm like!

Some kind of rabid animal with fleas and god knows what else snuggled up to your privates? Jesus, Billy.

Well it's no worse than some of the animals that 'ave been in your kegs lately, huh?

What?

You know what I'm on about – half the lasses in this joint go all weepy over you, how'd you fuckin' do it?

Never mind that, what about these driving lessons, you in or not?

Nope, driving lessons is the least of me worries right now. Say, you couldn't sub me could ya, seeing as how you're still flush?

On what terms?

The usual, ten per cent over and above, or maybe five per cent what with us being room buddies 'n' all?

So you can go home and buy a ferret?

Yeah.

And how in the fucking hell am I gonna repossess a ferret should the need arise?

Ah c'mon, it's your old mucker Billy you're dealing with now, not some fooking Frog!

So I lent him the cash and, on the eve of our days off, who should I see in the hotel bar living the hog's life with my fucking money than one Billy Shivers? That kid just never learned; money don't buy you love. I can't recall Billy ever telling me any more about the new ferret, but I do remember him telling me lots about pinball. Suddenly he was mad for it, the flippers, flashing lights, bells and whistles. Down there in some amusement arcade in his slippers going hard it, and all of his spare cash, and plenty more besides gobbled up by those machines.

Don't you have to be deaf, dumb and blind to play good pinball? I asked him one night as we stood side by side on the ranges.

Nah, it's in yer blood see, pinball is.

Maybe so, but it didn't do much for me. I had better shit to do than stand hunched over a pinball machine in the wee small hours. Like driving lessons. That headcase Fernando put me on to the instructor guy and the lessons were reasonably priced, although for some weird reason they were always conducted at night. Mr Frank, the instructor, was an old guy and he insisted on putting one hand on my leg, reassuringly I suppose. I told the saucier about this one morning and he looked at me rather quizzically.

Is it a manual? he asked me.

Of course, only girls drive automatics! Shit man!

Where'd you find out about this old letch? the saucier probed, as he burnt a reduction down to cinders.

Fernando, I told him, as acrid smoke began to enflame my nostrils.

Fucking hell, that Fernando's as bent as a forcemeat attachment – there's your answer!

You mean, Mr Frank might be . . .

Look Luiz, you little cocksucker, there's no might about it. Why'd you think you're driving around at night, in the dark, huh?

Getting my night vision, I told him.

Night vision my hairy bollocks, the only visions being had in that car are from Mr Frank as he visualizes your pecker in his hand, buddy!

Jesus, I thought those lessons were cheapish.

Dump that old pervert before the pack get a whiff of it okay, otherwise it'll be open slather on your arse, kid!

Fuck, just when I was getting confident with roundabouts and zebra crossings too, what a fucking bummer. It all made sense, Mr Frank telling me there were plenty of ways to get a licence on the cheap. Luckily the saucier was one of the good guys and he kept my accidental nocturnal adventures quiet – no wonder Fernando and his camp bosom-buddies had been lining up for chow all giving me the wink and leery smiles. A good woman would cure this predicament, and as there weren't any good ones available, I'd have to settle for a bad one, then dump her like a hot banana fritter as soon as the heat on me cooled off.

There are plenty of bad women hanging around the intestines of large hotels like garish tapeworms on the prowl for body heat, but not too many of them have principles low-slung enough to consider an apprentice chef as a decent catch. Josie, however, was one such girl, a fish-eyed, straggly-haired specimen who had slipped right through the trawl net along with her over-freckled twin Annie. They were the kind of evil-looking sisters horror film producers are always on the lookout for; both seriously in need of exorcism. I was no priest, but I was the next best thing.

I had no moves, had never needed them. But with girls such

as these it is not so much slick moves as movement itself that will have the desired effect. Girls like these are not used to being manhandled, not unless it is by some drunken uncle at a Christmas shindig. I had to choose one, no way did I require the services of both, and, having chosen, it was far easier to drag Josie to my stinking room than it was to drag my filthy laundry down to the basement on laundry day. All of this because of innuendo and money – fucking money causes way too many problems. I was better off without the damned stuff, surfing hopelessly from payday to payday. Maybe Billy had the right idea: spend it before you lose your bottle and start investing in your future, or worse, letting some raggy-arsed bird invest in it for you.

Who's that fooking tramp in our room? Billy asked me angrily. He had his dressing-gown on and was just back from the bathroom. I'd returned from popping down to the porter's room for essential supplies – such as smelling salts to arouse some kind of emotive response from the living zombie prostrate on my bed.

Her, oh, that's um . . . shit, what's her fucking name?

You're getting as bad as the rest of 'em. Say, she ain't into threesomes is she?

No fucking way. Or maybe she is Billy, lad, why don't you ask her?

Don't she 'ave a sister?

She does, and your point is?

Can you 'ook me up with her?

She's not the kind of girl who needs 'ooking up, Billy, all you gotta do is go down the TV room, take a hold of her cold slimy hand and lead her wherever you want. Once they're separated like this they're both as docile as stunned heifers. Look at this one? Go on, prod her with something, Jesus Billy lad, not that! Put that away you animal. Here, try this ... see, it's like I've just dug her up in the graveyard.

Without that awful stench the dead 'ave though ...

What?

That's what I heard, about the dead.

Say, if you're going down for the other one, can you take this one along with you, Billy lad?

You're finished with her?

Yup, there's a good film on TV in twenty minutes and I need a bath, I feel kind of ...

Crabby?

Oh god, please don't mention shellfish!

19.

Anarchy In The UK

Back at school, they had decided to treat us as young adults, which we undoubtedly were, by age if nothing else, and that was their mistake. It was time for trips, and that was a time all teachers feared the most. On the Monday I heard two of them talking out near the pig bins while some scrawny grunt was shovelling up leftover apple crumble.

This year is the absolute pits, one said between puffs on a pipe.

I agree comrade, ventured the other, all delinquents and perverts, god knows what state the profession is going to be in when these little bastards take charge!

First up was some kind of pre-dawn excursion to see fresh fish, when it was still actually fresh. Fishmongers rise at some ungodly hour and revel in the seminal stinks of fresh sea offal. The bus left at two thirty in the fucking morning, however it wasn't a major problem for us; we had been drinking since seven the previous night and had slept little.

Ye gods! the lecturer exclaimed when he first laid eyes upon us on that foggy morn, you can't get on a bus looking and smelling like that!

Generally, as you have surmised, the chef is ambivalent

about such matters as personal appearance, all that really concerns him is how fast he can reach a bar and he does not plan to be distracted from that task by appearing too interesting to the opposite sex. Although having said that, there are many kinds of women who seem unable to curtail their impulsiveness in throwing themselves at the most unkempt and pugnacious person at the bar, no matter the fall out. Who knows what carnal instinct drives these kinds of women; what exactly it is that stirs in them during the vampiric hours and compels them to seek out the intimacy of men who look disturbingly like Charlie Manson? And if anyone in a bar at that time of the day looks like Manson, then almost certainly it will be a chef not long from service. So we looked a rabble, and we smelled like swine, but so fucking what, eh?

At the markets we marched solemnly around vast crates of stinking fish that looked about as happy with their lot as we did. After several hours of this mind-numbing tour, we headed to the tasting room. There are some evil bastards in those fish joints, old men who can shell a fresh oyster quicker than either you or I can dry-retch. On a cold steel bench, heavy with moisture and liberally sprinkled with remnants of the shucker's business, they had lined up a couple of dozen oysters. It was not a pretty sight, not at five on a cold drizzly morning when you are rather badly hungover and the last thing you ate was Chinese fried rice some fourteen hours earlier. I could see people around me turning the colour of the fish we had just been kissing while others were emitting a low gut moan, the kind you hear from behind locked cubicle doors in bus terminal conveniences. One by one we stepped forward while the ruddy-faced host and a gaggle of teachers, rugged up against the chill like Dickensian characters, bombarded and baited us with abuse like the crowd used to do at ceremonial dippings.

Billy went before me. I studied his reaction with the keenest of interest; Billy was not what you might term a fresh-fish man. To his credit, however, he proved himself resilient in such matters, gulping down the mollusc with a spirited gusto and then belching rather disgustingly.

Fookin' great, he said in a manly fashion, much to the admiration of the mob.

Your roommate swallows then? some head said to me out of the side of his mouth.

He's renowned for it in the saunas, I replied.

And you, sweetmeats? my new friend continued.

That little fucker of yours gets anywhere near my mouth, brother, I'll bite it clean off.

I went up to the bench and took my delight, swallowed the gunk in one swig, and to be honest I have tasted worse; although right then I found it hard to remember anything that came close to a fresh-shucked oyster at five on a frigid morning. Maybe the oyster might live up to its reputation as a gourmand's and lover's delight in the splendid ambience of a top-class restaurant with fine claret at hand and some kind of accompaniments such as lemon and cocktail sauce – but not on a day such as this. We needed something wet, and after that many of us needed the fish market shithouses.

The highlight of our outing was to be the Hotel Olympia. It used to be at Earl's Court, before the place was overrun by expatriate antipodeans, that is. We were instructed to stroll around looking at all the many labour-saving and cost-effective advances that foreign manufacturing was enabling the average English hotel to utilize at a fifth of the price of the same goods from Sheffield. It was as tedious as stirring a consommé and as laborious as peeling carrots, but it was free. Many of us found a bar and gathered there to pool resources, thereby enabling most of us to drink our fill. After this, feeling in a far more salubrious frame of mind, we fanned out, like field mice in a cornfield, to fill our bags with as many free goods and brochures that we could find – and indeed many items that were neither free nor intended as promotional material.

After several hours of this we were all gathered up ready to enter the Salon, where some kind of gladiatorial contest for chefs from around the isles was going on, the contestants wearing medals and ribbons as if they had fought in the Falklands. After supplying the mandatory urine samples we left the great arena and trooped back out into the early dusk onto a bus.

An hour later we stopped for grub, and by that stage we were ready to eat. You would think that most owners of fair-to-middling establishments would be terrified by the thought of having to feed twenty-odd chefs and their escorts, but such is not the case at all. Chefs are the easiest people in the world to feed: you would be better off cooking for a dozen chefs than you would be cooking the Christmas dinner for a whole swathe of your extended family. Chefs are simple people, in fact many of them are the simplest people I have ever known. If it is hot and wet, a chef will eat it – and in times of drought, even if it is dry and cold. This is why you will always find chefs smacking their chops in some greasy spoon café, or in one of those motorway truck-stops, pawing or drooling, sometimes both, over a plastic menu with tomato ketchup stains. For there is no greater joy than being served a full English breakfast at any hour of the day or night by some hirsute brute of a cook covered in fat splatters: seeing those two grease-riddled eggs, like eyes on a squid, squirming on your plate; looking at that crispy bacon, the over-cooked sausage and eighteen pieces of toast. A meal like that can almost make you feel proud to be British. Almost.

We rolled back into town several hours later, exhausted by the excitement and culinary thrills and spills. Billy had been sick again and another boy had been thrown off the bus a few miles out of town for continually setting alight his own anal gases … The lights were on in our prison, and none of us had made a clean break, although there had been ample opportunities.

Billy was still sick when we got up to our garret. A sickly green colour had taken to him around the gills and he was retching at every kind of sloppy food I mentioned. Maybe he had some kind of food poisoning?

The tramp I'd laid turned up at our door, claiming to be pregnant. I took her down to the porter's lounge, to see what could be done.

When I got back a couple of hours later Billy was in a coma, still dressed, as motionless and as pale as fresh road kill. Jesus, this'll look fucking good on my CV, I thought – dead boy in room. Okay, enough of that shit, so I picked him up and walked him around a bit, like they do in movies when some junkie has OD'd. It works, too, because within fifteen minutes Billy was back to consciousness moaning about whippets and so on. It had been a close call, that's for sure. I stayed up all night lest he slip into a stupor again and never awake. This is the kind of room buddy that I am.

I didn't see too much of the tramp after I'd talked to the porters; they made a few calls and I ended up in their debt – again – which entailed many nights pleading with the sous, playing Duce while we awaited the Duce's replacement, to let me stay back and do the night tray.

What the fuck are you up to Luiz, you little shit? the faux Duce grilled me one night as I helped him into his mink stole.

Me boss? Nothing, just doing my bit for in-house staff relationships.

You're not feeding those arsehole porters the good shit are you? By god, if you are I'll yank your balls off myself and casserole them!

Me! Hell no! You know me better than that, boss!

I know you all right, and what about this lass you've gotten up the duff?

A case of mistaken identity, boss, I'm not the settling down kind.

Are you going home this weekend? Your folks keep pestering F&B, claimed they haven't set eyes on you for months.

I am, boss, promise.

After the Duce had stumbled out to a waiting taxi I piled up the night porter's tray with the good stuff, and enough of it to please Lucifer himself.

20.

Metal Guru

My mother didn't recognize me at the depot.

Hi Mum! I said, after having crept up on her from behind, just like I'd learned from the SAS boys in the cold larder.

Oh my Lord! she exclaimed, not at the surprise, but at my appearance; I had tumbled a long way from the fresh-faced young boy she had sobbed over a year or so ago. I had long raggy hair that I'd tied back with a piece of shredded tea towel, a denim jacket covering an all-but-bare chest and, for some unknown reason, I was still wearing my chef's pants and clogs.

Are you due back tonight? she asked me.

I'm on a forty-eight hour pass, I told her. Is The Ship still open do you think?

It's almost midnight, darling, public houses aren't open at that hour down here, and where is your luggage?

Luggage? I'm not going on a cruise you know, besides, I've got gear at home . . .

Oh, I gave that stuff to Oxfam.

So I don't have clothes at home?

At least you're still referring to it as home, darling. I'll find you some clothes, you're about my size by the sight of you – and food, don't you ever eat in that hotel?

They don't let you, Mum, the bastards.

Oh! and that mouth of yours!

In the car heading homeward, my mother insisted on giving me the rundown of family goings-on, and of the crank calls she'd been receiving from some foul-mouthed girl claiming to be my wife. As if, I told her, you know I'm not that kind of boy, eh?

On the train back to the grindstone, wearing my mum's jeans, I found myself pretty flush. Not only had I again won the biannual family table-tennis tournament in a canter, but had also fleeced the old man of a considerable sum at three-card brag, and employed my usual subtle stand-over tactics to coerce my younger brother into parting with his pocket money. These are a few of the many life skills you acquire while whittling away the hours at HM's pleasure. There are others, of course, but we needn't delve into those just yet. Suffice to say when the old man checked his safe there would be all hell to pay. Yes indeed, I was an all-round nice guy, a shining exemplar no less to those peers of mine who still lived at home and struggled along on their paper-round money.

School dragged on like a stay of execution; some fell by the wayside, like those with an aversion to regulated timetables are apt to do. Golden Brown and Miss J eloped one cold afternoon, just leapt straight into the big man's Citroën and headed south, or was it west? To be sure, they wouldn't get too far in a car like that. My old fella had owned a brand new Citroën once, a dark blue number with a tan roof, one of those mothers that raised itself up and down on hydraulic suspension. That car smelt mighty fine until the day its brakes went kerr-ping and it ended up upside down in a cow field – no sir, you can't get far in a Citroën.

After a few weeks I felt I had a handle on that school gig. I was coasting, and Helmut the friendly host at the Just Wormed Dachshund had my ale pulled fifteen minutes before I showed up each day like dewy milk bottles on a doorstep. One night, however, while tending some menial chore in the large white temple I was summarily summoned to see the faux Duce in his private quarters, and was escorted there by two KPs wearing military armbands. I smelt a shift in the air; an odour of something foul on the wind that blew in through the back doors.

Take a seat, the big man told me – and by Christ you never got to sit in the great man's office, not unless you were soon to be executed. So I sat there watching while the Duce calmly flipped through the kind of magazine that graphically depicted nubile Scandinavian girls getting it on with well-hung German shepherds. Maybe the Duce was going to sack me; maybe he had a part for me in one of his upcoming film productions? Christ Almighty, I just wish the guy would get it over with . . .

Luiz, Luiz, Luiz, he moaned, as if we'd just enjoyed some kind of intimate coitus. What the hell's happened to you?

Yeah well, it was one of those questions you're unsure whether to respond to or not, like: Now then shitface, where were you on the night of . . . Well, I'm sure you catch my drift. The thing in these situations is not to be overcome by some kind of premature ejaculatory emotion, but instead to hunker down, take the ticket and enjoy the ride – take a shit or get off the damned bowl. Indeed, many strange and bizarre outcomes flew through my otherwise vacant head like arrows on a battlefield as the Big Cheese contemplated his next move like some grand chess master on BBC2.

As I felt the sweat break like a dose of hives, I got that ugly intense feeling most usually associated with a dead-end alley not far from a pub on a rotten Saturday evening. Finally the

Duce slid a piece of paper over the desk toward me; bad thoughts of forced confessions came to mind.

It's very sad, he began, his big old bloodhound eyes far too big and bloodshot for my liking, so very sad indeed. Shit, my own old man had grassed me up for burglary! But no, as I glanced down at the piece of paper I instantly recognized a name thereon – my nemesis, one Jean Paul Bumfrisker. Just what the hell had that demented old bastard gone and done now, expelled me?

GODDAMNIT! the Duce suddenly roared while smacking his desk with one big bovine hoof and sending his miniature port glasses from Bratislava all over the goddamned show.

Stay calm, I heard myself saying, you've been in worse situations than this; remember that time in the showers at ...

The chief wiped his hand across his head like Kurtz and then told me the whole sorry saga, just like I knew he would.

There were some faceless and heartless 'men' upstairs, vile hideous creatures concerned only with the fine calibrations of the profit/loss ledger, who were not too keen on continuing to pay school fees for some kind of booze-head wastrel.

Indeed, I thought, isn't it always the way?

And look at you! the Duce continued, and what, by Christ, is that dangling from your lughole? I fingered the safety pin casually, for this was no time for histrionics.

That? I said. That's just a token.

And then there's this girl!

There is *no* girl boss, that's all gossip – you know what those chamberbitches are like.

Good Christ Almighty! the Duce shrieked, causing the two arm-banded KPs to burst in like storm troopers on the eve of a putsch. The Duce waved them away and we continued our friendly discourse. What it all boiled down to was the fact that Jean Paul thought I had great potential, and to be sure hadn't other people once said the very same thing? My family doctor when he gave that character reference in court on that sultry afternoon? My old PE teacher when I applied for a free transfer from rugby to girls' hockey?

Regrettably, however, that much-anticipated potential wasn't manifesting itself, something was distracting me and as it stood I was on the very slippery slope sign-posted 'failure'.

I didn't have the gall, of course, to tell the chief that I had a burgeoning career as a pool hustler up at the Shit-faced Dachshund; that Herr Helmut thought I could make the pro circuit, spend my days lounging around seedy hotels in Spain drinking sangria and watching old movie re-runs and the balmy evenings hustling lobster-red on-the-run expatriates for spends.

That I was taking on all comers up there for princely sums, and the status it afforded me was cramping up my culinary-arts learning time. The Duce told me in no uncertain terms that if I failed the exam the hotel would cut me loose, toss me out on the street like a cheap bum. No one was interested in having to fork out that much cash on a loser. It was an ugly scene as I sat there looking suitably admonished while the sous gave me the ins and outs of the financial side of things and reminisced about some zany kitchen version of the Night of the Long Knives.

That was when I suddenly realized what they'd all meant, the warden, the magistrate, my old fella, when they'd prophesied that someday I'd get The Book thrown at me – because the sous chucked one and it hit me square on the noggin.

Get out my sight! he scolded me, and don't come back until you can recite the bloody repertoire from Appareils to Welsh Rarebit, and get that god-awful thing out of your ear before what's left of your brain gets gangrene – you look like a goddamned punk.

I guessed that that wasn't a compliment.

How'd you go kiddo? Billy asked me, when I got back upstairs.

Just the usual, I told him.

Is that lug of yours infected? he continued. I looked at it in the mirror. Jesus H., that's all I needed.

I'll be back in a minute, I told him.

Where you goin'? Can I come? Billy always wanted to follow me around, not that I minded, it was just that having a kid wearing a cardigan and slippers following you around kinda cramped what little style you had.

Look, I'm only going down to the porter's lounge, to get some Dettol and some cotton-wool, okay?

Can I come?

Why the hell not, but lose the slippers, okay?

What's fooking wrong with me slippers?

Shit, Billy, don't you ever wonder why you don't get laid?

I think about it . . .

Well, think harder, eh?

Are you gonna get sacked?

Who said that?

Dianne, that one who's got the hots for you, the one with the motherly hips.

I don't know any Dianne, apart from the sauce, you know, the one with a base of reduced shallots, French mustard, fonds brun, gherkin jus, cognac . . .

You really know your sauces!

Too fucking true.

Anyhow, the Duce's message must have struck a golden chord somewhere in the subconscious mind, because before I knew it I was back climbing up the ladder of success. Time flew by and the seasons changed, many otherwise warped notions altered their perspective in my mind and many things – like safety pins for one – found themselves again being used for their intended purposes. The Duce was happy too, and occasionally would pat me tenderly on the bottom like a priest does his favourite choirboys after a hymn well sung. At college I began to espouse the virtues of great men – the men who wrote The Book by candlelight before the last of their memories and knowledge faded forever. This time around I would stick to the straight and narrow, but then again, I'd often said much the same before …

21.

I Really Love Your Tiger Feet

The king was gone and the kitchen that Billy and I returned to after another fling with college was not the kitchen we had fallen into head first through no fault of ours. The appointment of a new Duce can take time. Maybe the first choice had been scared off by his initial glimpse of the brigade he was to inherit, or perhaps he had obligations to another employer, a woman or an irate pimp.

What remained of the old brigade was all aflutter with tidbits of information. People kept mentioning faces they had recognized wandering the grand halls. Isn't he that fuckhead Gary, the one who beats his wife and drinks pure meth? That kind of thing – we were beset by head jobs, nutcases, cranks and the usual assortment of fly-by-nighters and reprobates who normally fling themselves into such hotpots like pigeons into jet propellers. Management are normally pretty savvy when it comes to weeding out such conmen, although that hasn't stopped the odd lunatic from grabbing the top job at Claridges now and again.

Change can be uplifting, the metaphorical new broom that might just sweep all of the old resentment, frustration and mundane away with one foul swoop, so to speak. I was hoping for the new broom, because if the sous ended up squatting permanently on the top perch, nothing much would change.

I have always had a preference for the novel approach, I am all for change. In big kitchens, this viewpoint is not the norm, however. Many of the brigade had vested interests in seeing one of their own promoted, as they believed, and quite often rightly so, that then their life would become more comfortable. In a big kitchen familiarity does not breed contempt – it breeds complacency.

So we waited, stood around like butt-idle morons for the white smoke to drift from the hotel chimney as a sign that the new Duce had been elected. Money changed hands, although as is the way in the industrial kitchen, much of it was by way of markers and other people's still unpaid debts – do you know it was a chef who came up with the idea of buying debts? Interesting.

Anyhow, the brigade sweated it out and management played it very tight-lipped; even the porters couldn't grab an inside track on the matter. Finally, we learnt, the new king had accepted the throne and was due to commence his duties as ruler of the kingdom the following Monday. For many, it was a long and fraught weekend, but not for me; I was on the fish, covering for that pervert Bumble, and as such I felt it my duty to pitch in and attempt to right the wrong that the fish boys felt had unfairly fallen into their midst.

On the fish it's an ultra-violet kinda life. There ain't no room in the bunkhouse for lard-arses and slack-jaws down there in the hole; down there every day is fucking Nam. There are scales, lots of 'em, but the scales of justice are not always accurate. I liked the fish section, some didn't, Billy was one, but I always rather enjoyed the gutting and skinning of fish, the barbarity of hurling live crustaceans into boiling vats and the thrill of untying crabs and watching them fight it out to the death in the fish room while we wagered on the winner. There is never a dull moment on the fish section; the same cannot be said of the veg. To be sure it is messy rotten work and there are many hazards: sharp teeth, razor-edged fins, claws, those ragged bits all over lobsters – while a fish cut is the worst of all, prone to bad infection; fish might live in water but on the whole they are filthy creatures. But all in all it is good wholesome work and the fish boys are fun to be around, everything comes their way, from bisques to chowders and from stocks to broths, they are a happy acid crew as they wade knee-deep in guts and roe searching for just one more useable fillet to get them out of the shit bog. On the fish there is always a Beach Boys or Eagles tune playing, maybe a Stones too that's had its lyrics altered: *I see a line of eels and they're all painted . . .* Maybe a Mac song or two to wind it all down. The boys sport dapper earrings and blond-tinted hair and they know the difference between a Dublin bay prawn and a Channel shrimp. Theirs is a fast-paced environment where everything depends upon split-second timing, there is no turning back once the moules hit the marinière, and if the docket has been called too early then you are skating on very thin ice. And this is why the fish section always runs its own gimp. The fish boys are a clique, a real gang, just like you find on street corners in East LA. Sometimes they will all take to wearing the same adornments, perhaps a coloured necktie or different coloured clogs to distinguish them from the rest of the brigade; fish boys like to stand out in a crowd.

They are not lugubrious types by nature, but they hold the fish up as sacrosanct and woe betide anyone foolish enough to belittle their daily rituals. Let us never forget that we are a nation of fisher folks first and foremost and this is why the perch was oft regarded as a wise and worldly creature – oh hang on, sorry, not the perch – the John Dory! And while we're on the subject of fish, just what the hell happened to the smelts, the chads and the lampreys? Yes, that is a good question indeed.

So, the hunt for the new Duce had ended and we the brigade held our collective breaths. The fulcrum had been breached and everyone in management seemed quite happy, skipping here and there holding hands like schoolgirls on a summer's morn. Monday skulked around looking all dishevelled and moody – Mondays can be like that in the kitchen. Monday is delivery day, the day crude and indignant delivery people bung your shit as far from the backdoor as they can and then flee in terror. This Monday was no different – the raspberries had slid from their tray and were every fucking where. A tall kid was with me, but he was whingeing.

Can I go for a shit before we start hauling? he asked me in his whiny voice.

You're not going fucking anywhere, I told him sternly, there's still about a hundred raspberries missing, slide under that skip and see what you can find.

There might be bugs under it.

Bugs? Of course there's fucking bugs under it, which is why you need to get those fucking raspberries out before they get eaten.

So under he went, like a marlin fighting on the end of a long line. Back in the kitchen a crowd had gathered, a whole herd of white like a hailstorm in July, the new Duce had taken control and from now on the whole place would go through cataclysmic change – or so I hoped.

Who is it? I asked one of the pastry geeks. He was filing his nails indulgently and had all four of the different coloured biros sticking out of his breast pocket.

Never seen him before, he replied indignantly. They say he's a real bastard.

I left him there, stuck in a miasma of confectionary complacency, and strode over to where the pack had gathered to pump the new Duce's hand – and for some of them this would be the second to last time that they ever did, next time it would be to say goodbye.

As the thicket of thickheads cleared, I had to look twice, surely it couldn't be ... ye gods, of all of the flukiest twists that fate could spring. I put my hand out and the Duce took it warmly.

Never thought you'd see me again huh, you little runt? he said rather affectionately.

Nope, thought I'd seen the back of you! I joked, as the rest of the brigade seethed behind me with contempt, and most likely fear.

Billy about? the new Duce asked, and I told him that Billy was on his RDO.

The new Duce smiled. I'll get settled then come over to the office, fill me in on this joint, okay?

O fucking K, boss, I told him enthusiastically, and as I turned around, twenty pairs of nervous eyes burned into mine.

You know the Duce? the veg chef asked me as he clung to the mixer for stability.

Know him? I replied, well I ought to, he used to be mine and Billy's sous chef!

Alan, our old sous, had snuck in under the radar.

What a bloody turn up, huh? I told Billy excitedly that afternoon after he'd come back from the record store with some new jive record.

Fooking great! he told me while he hung his just dry-cleaned white suit back up, maybe now some of these wankers'll get the boot, huh?

I fucking hope so, I said. I did too, there is no time for empathy when the big wheels begin to turn. When that happens it is every man for himself and in the kitchen we never adhere to the rule of women, children and transvestites first – if they want to go first they'd better be damned well prepared for grizzly hand-to-hand combat.

I had never seen so many anally retarded spooks so well attired; gone were the gratuitous self-adornments, the bones, the fish eyes, the necklaces, the earrings, and in their place were pristine white jackets double-buttoned right to the top. Correctly tied neckties and razor-edged hats. For once, the place resembled a kitchen of old – even the fish boys had taken a bath and run a comb through their hair. I hardly recognized anyone. A new Duce can have such a dramatic effect that he or she can, quite literally, scare the living bejesus out of a brigade that has grown fat and incompetent. And to be sure, there was plenty of lard for the new Duce to shave off in this gin palace. He knew it too, because only the day before I had given him an oration on the subject matter at hand, and of course he was more than pleased with my treachery. The Duce, any Duce, is a person whom no one should ever trust – the Duce can be shaking your hand one minute and your throat the next; they are passive-aggressive people and they toil under the most extreme pressures – but the one thing all Duces share is the adoration of a supergrass.

Okay, so it went against all of my inherent principles, as I was not, and still am not, renowned as the proverbial snake in the woodpile. However, there are some situations where even the most ardent abuser of authority must choose to rub against the grain and come up smelling as sweet as Chanel No. 5. And so I did. In circumstances such as the ones I am describing to you now, it was imperative that the opportunity for spiteful retribution and self-advancement be seized. You are never the chosen one for long, and as such you must butter your croissant while there is still butter in the pot.

The cull started, and as brutal as these events are to the bystander, things are all undertaken in the name of progress. The Duce wanted some fresh meat around him, some young blood, and within a week the national magazines were carrying positions vacant adverts for our very hotel. I liked it, I liked watching the revolving door revolve; out with the old, in with the new.

And by Christ, I remember telling Billy as we watched the daily procession, look at the state of some of these jerks, huh?

That fooker looks like a right head job, Billy told me as we studied a half-caste character with a mop of hair that looked like it had been dunked in a tar pit. Trust the Duce to hire a freak like that . . . The times, they were certainly a changin'.

22.

Ballroom Blitz

Vinnie came to us from Liverpool, and he was the genuine article, sump water pumping through what remained of his arterial system, and a mop of lank, black curly hair that hung over his face like grapes in Babylon. Vinnie quickly became known as Yogi, and then YG, a kitchen name he earned due to the fact he always responded to a request or direct order with the words 'yeah great'. Maybe we ought to have christened him The Sperminator, as YG went through the female populous faster than Schumacher can a chicane. He possessed a quality that many women, and especially hospitality women, found irresistible: rank crudeness.

Apart from his allure to the opposite gender, YG was all but single-handedly responsible for the distressed denim and designer-sneaker industries that we know and love today. Not to mention being at the very forefront of the hydroponic movement, what with his nocturnal tinkerings down in the pot wash. He had developed a well-loved routine for his Lee's. First he would spend an afternoon swimming in them, then lay on the beach until they dried on him. After that he'd return to the kitchen, traipsing sand and seaweed everywhere, peel off the form-fit jeans and sling them into the first pot he could find, fill it with a mix of water and bleach, and boil those mothers until they were virtually white, standing there in the kitchen in just his yellowy smalls – when he bothered to wear any, that was. Sometimes he'd just wrap a discarded apron around himself and the whole place knew what YG's arse looked like. Next he would dry his jeans in a pastry oven alongside the meringues. Finally, during service – and no matter how frenetic it was, YG always seemed to have ample time for skylarking and shenanigans – he could be seen carefully cutting slashes into his denim with someone else's blade, and usually not even on a fucking chopping board. YG was a person completely comfortable with both the style and pace of life in a big kitchen. Where others lost their heads, YG would always remain calm and in control. He was a committed substance abuser, of course – all of the most level-headed ones are – and as dedicated to self-abuse as Sid Vicious. When he couldn't afford decent gear YG had no qualms about using the Vim, and that is above and beyond the call of duty even in the junk industry. Punk and YG fitted together like a tongue and groove joint and he brought to us, at least, the very essence of rebellion.

It had been a very long time since I had shoplifted, and in fact the thrill of the act had long since faded in my mind. But not in YG's. The guy was a klepto and we couldn't go to a shop without YG stuffing gear into his ratty old overcoat, which he insisted on wearing over his shorts even in summer. One afternoon he self-pierced his own top lip with a safety pin from the first aid box and it turned septic. No worries there, it was just a matter of popping down to the chemist and picking up some supplies – literally. If YG hadn't been a chef he would have been a frequent offender and living in institutions. Cookery rescued him from that fate and gave him a better quality of life, albeit an only slightly better one.

I recall turning up for staff tea one evening after I had

watched the kids' programs, to discover YG bent over a bubbling cauldron of something that reeked.

What the fuck's that? I asked him, and YG was happy to advise me that it was the time of year when he gave his socks and jocks a good boil.

You know we're using that fucking pot for cauli tonight don't you?

YG just shrugged. Yeah, fucking great, eh?

And then there was Herman, a different breed completely to YG but nonetheless intriguing. Herman had a look that reminded you of a young Goebbels, what with the round glasses, the neatly clipped hair and the ironed denim shirts. He came from Worcestershire, up where they grow the asparagus and people are well-educated.

Herman was a pastry nut, a real choux pastry geek. He was the first pastry chef I had formed an acquaintance with – most normally those geeks stay close together like wolf packs in the North Atlantic.

Herman was a member of the intelligentsia and management loved it, the quintessential poet-chef, a scholar: a learned and caring human being, and, of course, the women swooned over him. Women do this, I have found; they are creatures who prefer men of extremes, either they will be unable to resist hurling themselves at a drunken cavalier with a mouth like a guttersnipe and a desperado appearance, or they will go all gooey over the poet and his tortured soul.

There is little hope for anyone in-between; women are rarely interested in normal men. In the big hotel you are able to study life, the evolutionary cycle and the fickle whims of the fairer sex, although to be honest even if you are a studier, you will never comprehend them – far better to be a fancier, I think. Still, both YG and H had their techniques. YG was a crash and bang merchant and he lived for the immediate thrill and pondered not the consequences. YG was a chef's chef, I suppose, the kind ready, willing and able to let some lay he'd found pay her own cab fare home, whereas H paid careful attention to what he allowed to slip between his sheets. He was not the kind of man who was interested in quantity, quality was always his watchword, and where YG was content to live and die by the sword, H was more interested in controlling his fate by way of contraceptive protection and by comprehensively vetting prospective bedmates.

It is rare to find such a person in a big throbbing white machine – a man of due diligence and petit mannerisms, unafraid to tackle subjects that most chefs run a mile from faster than a dopehead sprinter. As I have said, Herman was fond of the poets, and when time was dragging, as it did when the cocktail bar was full and the waiters were feverishly organizing seating arrangements, H would always have something interesting to impart into the otherwise vacant minds of those around him.

Both YG and H scored well at the weekly hotel disco. They had perfected the technique of the hunt. Not all of us were so enabled in the deadly art of ensnaring a bedmate for the night, or even a part thereof. No sir, apprentice chefs don't do well in such a competitive environment; the fresh meat always attracts the biggest worms, and we apprentices were invariably left to slug it out over the mutton dressed as lamb, those middle-aged spinsters bedecked in ritzy jewellery who smelt like mothballs. But there's always a chance, even in the most desperate of situations, a chance that you'll get five minutes of post-pubescent fumbling and a shot at premature ejaculation – nothing ventured, nothing gained, I guess.

Anyhow, down on the heaving dance floor there is nothing

more comical, and indeed unnerving, than witnessing holidaying Britons, their usual reserve and inhibition busted by cheap cocktails and house white, up and stomping around a well-buffed ballroom. It is like watching the ritual mating of orangutans, and the British above all other nationalities insist on dancing while still clutching their drinks – as if in fear that some waiter will remove the half-empty glass before they have the chance to suck back those precious dregs where the high alcohol content lies. The women are worse, like whirling dervishes as they spin out of control and fall clumsily into the string section of the quartet on stage. There is something rather ugly – the result of a combination of age, free alcohol and music – that stirs in otherwise genteel women on holidays. No sooner do the house lights fall and the band strikes up, than they're casting off their inhibitions along with their fake furs.

There is more mayhem, however, further down, below the grand ballroom, in the basement; that is where on summer evenings mad shit happens, and the drink prices increase every half hour.

The house disco is what I refer to, and sweet Jesus it was a debauched spectacle, never more so than when a posse of shit-faced chefs straight from the closest public bar crashed it in the wee hours like a gang of thugs high on ether. It has always been a bilious affair, the discothèque, a place where everything is fake, where the girls seem happy to dance with themselves and the boys quite content to watch, up until a certain point. Darwin would have been quite at home roaming around the dance floor with his slide rule and magnifying glass, measuring craniums and inspecting ear canals. At the bars you find rows of chefs three-deep studying the talent, eyeing off the super-troopers, space cadets, numb nuts and easy lays. These wasters are all hard cases and they are there in the main for any spot of business that might or might not occur – the rumble, as it were, and of course they are giving everyone else the needle in the hope of provoking trouble.

The bar at the house disco in a swanky hotel is an environment fraught with perils – and I, for one, always sent Billy to get our sups.

In Britain of course we are creatures of habit, and that is why disco still goes through its torturous throes most Saturday nights across the land, and why in the curdling hours, gangs of ripped-to-the-tits chefs still find it good clean fun to stomp around on the dance floor doing the monster mash with a lager in one hand and someone else's wife in the other.

Those places smell rank, a few hundred sweating foreigners going at it hard to 'Children of the Revolution' is neither pretty nor aromatic, and by the time 'Stayin' Alive' hits the decks there are firemen everywhere desperately trying to clear the exits. Discos are highly combustible places and a casually discarded fag can bring the roof down pretty damned quick. The only saviour disco has, and especially the hotel disco, is that the bar staff have few reservations about serving alcohol to minors. In fact they encourage it, and why not at such marked-up prices?

Billy, naturally, lived for the disco. It was all he could talk about the whole week beforehand. He would hope that that cute little Danish number turned up again, that we weren't kept on late duty, that his suit came back from the dry clean in time, that those two zits on his nose were ready to pop before the off, that maybe he could find someone to sub him a few spends, and that the crazy old bitch who'd manhandled his goods last Saturday didn't turn up again – he was sure he had liver spots sprouting below decks already.

Inevitably, the cute little Danish number would turn out to be a Finnish boy, Billy wouldn't have enough cash to buy a tonic water, someone would puke on his suit again, and the old bitch with the freezer-like paws would be at him as though the last time she'd seen good meat was on the slab at the funeral home.

These are just a few of the pitfalls that beset disco. Still, there are many in the industry who couldn't care less about such trifling matters, like foreign waiters . . . and me, people who are quite happy to schmooze the night away with one eye firmly on the quick and clean kill, the hospitality equivalent of *Lord of the Flies*.

You learn to seize your opportunities. You learn to dance – if, that is, you want to compete in the mating rut – and if you can boogie, you can bed, is the adage that applies to hotel discos. But by dancing, I do not mean twirling about fully tanked up wearing a white suit. That is a sure-fire recipe for complete failure.

I tried to teach Billy to dance, down in the empty ballroom, but by god, he was as stiff and as awkward as a forty-year-old virgin.

Loosen up, I told him, swivel those fucking hips!

I ain't gor fooking hips, only girls 'ave got hips.

Bullshit! Look at mine huh? Here, feel these babies, go on . . . put one hand on each and feel my moves.

No fooking thanks, I'll just watch . . .

Yeah, well, I tried. It's just that dancing is simple to some people and terrifyingly technical to others – but when you see ten Swedish girls dancing alone on a dance floor, you can either stay at the bar with your cronies leering drunkenly, or head for the action. The worst they can do is laugh at you contemptuously, right? That's what I always told Billy. Get in there, lad! I told him, but more often than not, his legs would fail him.

And that can happen to the best of us, now and again . . .

23.

The Golden Age Of Rock 'n' Roll

On one occasion I was dispatched to the laundry by a very angry Duce. He was unhappy that his bundle of clean gear had not yet been delivered, and he took the opportunity to send me down there to unearth just what the fuck was going on – he knew he could trust a punk like me to do his bidding. He had an important meeting with a financier in just under an hour and wished to look the consummate professional, for once at least. When the Duce selects you to run an errand you feel privileged, especially when you are also getting into the bargain a chit to vacate some heinous chore such as peeling asparagus.

Happy with my lot, I rode the elevator down to the sewers. It ground to a shaky halt and I yanked open the outer cage door. From there it was a reasonable hike to the laundry catacombs. The Duce would not worry overly about my whereabouts so long as I arrived back with his gear in time to permit him to shit, shower and shave.

As I weaved my way around the snaking corridors, following the smell of starch and washing powder, my few precious care-free moments of freedom were spoiled by a ghastly sight, a sight no big hotel apprentice should have to witness not long after having gulped down eight eggs and nine slices of hog for breakfast. The bales had caught my eye because I knew damned well that the iron maiden in the laundry would tell me with a malicious smile that the Duce's whites were secreted deep in one of those very bundles, still awaiting unpacking by some muscle-heavy goon short on grey matter. All of those worries, however, flew from my mind when I glimpsed what was behind the bales – well, going on behind them actually. Two waiters were engaged in what I believe the Romans used to call fellatio, the Romans always used beautiful-sounding words, words that themselves create a kind of oral pleasure, so to speak. Try starting your day saying fellatio twenty times very sensually while you're in the shower and you'll see what I mean.

One waiter was eagerly gobbling the other's dog, while the other enjoyed it. Or at least, looked as if he were enjoying it. Pleasures such as these usually take place in the privacy of people's homes, or failing that, around the back of railway stations or on the promenade late at night, and no one worries about them because such matters fall neatly into the file marked 'what the eye doesn't see'. They were lunch waiters, because the breakfast stroke lunch waiter is the most brazen of the species. What is the protocol in such situations anyhow? Should one retire discreetly or perhaps cough nervously and carry on pretending not to have seen? If we are splitting hairs, then I guess technically these two cocksuckers, if you'll excuse my directness, *were* at home, after all, they did live in the place.

They used to have spittoons in grand hotels and I figured out why right at that moment of maturity. Anyhow, I walked quite briskly past the scene and left the boys to it, only I couldn't help but think that within the hour those very lips might be kissing the back of a maiden's dainty hand in the hope of earning a bigger tip or a room number.

I was right anyhow, the Duce's gear was still to be unloaded and that left me with two more problems than I'd had fifteen minutes ago. Problems have a way of multiplying fast in the big hotel. By then I had a rapport going with the laundry girls, who had taken to mothering me a little. I was a gay little thing, always one for the slipped-in compliment on a new hairdo or shade of lipstick. I told them not to bother unpacking the bale, I'd do it – but, as I bade my farewells, they all began tittering. I am not a fan of the collective twitter, when you hear that, you can bet that something foul is afoot.

What? I asked them.

They asked me if I'd been to the stillroom yet that day, and I replied that I hadn't – well, I ought to, they told me, everyone was talking about it. What 'it'?

My problems were breeding faster than weevils, should I get the Duce's gear or should I detour up to the stillroom? Jesus H. I went up to the stillroom, hesitantly, where I encountered yet more twittering and a crowd. Some crazy bitch had posted up an 'Ode to Luiz' on the stillroom wall, a very graphic one too. Ye gods; the Duce's dirty linen and mine had become entangled, metaphorically speaking, and I ripped that muck off the wall pretty damned fast, this kind of thing is slander, or is it libel? I didn't know, but I knew someone who would, god willing I would survive this whole mess. And in the kitchen, I could hear the Duce shrieking my name . . .

Did I go and tell the big man I hadn't acquired his gear? That was question number one. Question number two was whether or not I told the boys on the line what I'd just been witness to? And question number three was whether or not the heads on the line had seen that crazy bitch's hate mail – hmm, ponderous, onerous, conundrum.

I would just have to face the music. It was after all, the golden age of rock 'n' roll.

There is no virtue, freedom or even truth in a big kitchen, and almost everyone is a slave, even the Duce himself. He cannot allow the reins to slip, to fall into the hands of a man who might perform better than he himself. He hangs on at all cost and the more desperate he becomes the more savage his backlash; it is the same with women, and at college, where we were due back for practical exams.

At cookery school, the French teachers hated our guts, and we hated theirs right back. We little souls would do our best to make vinaigrette that matched up to our French teacher's wet dreams – but alas, more often than not we would fail through miserable impotency. Monsieur Alex, the cold larder teacher, would come around with his little silver tasting spoon and a cherubic-looking boy who carried a towel and a bowl of sacrosanct gin. The good monsieur would taste your dressing, maybe your saliva too, and then his face would contort as if he had just taken strychnine; immediately he would spit out the obnoxious liquid into the bowl and wipe his face and his spoon with the towel. After this he would abuse you thoroughly in French and maybe you could pick up a few key words like 'Anglais' and 'mère', something along the lines of you being an English pig-dog with a mother from the whorehouse. It was stirring stuff, enough to convince even the most ambivalent of patriots to grab up a Union Jack and run around the streets looking for Europeans to cudgel. Some people took it better than others; I for example took it better than Billy, who always became irate that his parentage and heritage were being blasphemed.

So what? I would tell him out on the milk crates, the guy is only doing his best to make us chefs and they see things differently across the Channel, just like they do up your way, kiddo. Why can't you just chill for Christ's sake, here, have a Gitane, these things'll kill you in half the time it takes

English weed, you can get them discount from Monsieur Gabriel.

Fuck that shit, Billy would retort angrily. I didn't come down here to be fooking abused by Froggies.

None of us did, but that was our lot. Billy was having a rough time, what with the culmination of our fiendish plot to snatch a cocktail barman and torture him until he squealed about to come to a pus-filled head. And as for me, I was deep in the fire on all sides, under constant attack from my peers, lecturers, and two insane sisters from way north of the great divide who somehow believed I was the Antichrist.

I had to go and see Helen of Tyneside, the head chambermaid, to plead my case.

Look, I told her quite sternly, this kind of crap has got to stop, those witches are ruining my otherwise good reputation!

Howay kidda, she told me, you do the crime you do the time, like.

That's just the point! There's been no crime!

It's only your word versus theirs, pet, why not do the decent thing and make an honest woman out of one of 'em, you choose . . .

Are you fucking mad? Marry one of them? And bring up some dumb waiter's bastard?

What about engagement then? A token of appeasement?

No fucking way, why don't you just offload those nutcases?

Nay pet, those are two of me best cleaners!

Look, if you don't do something I'll have to poison them.

24.

I Will Survive

There would be many other tributaries for both Billy and I to doggie paddle across, but for now it was the kidnapping that occupied our minds. If you have ever seen *Deliverance* then you will appreciate fully that in some cases of injustice, those who have had the injustice committed against them are hot for a reverse fixture. But not Billy, his initial anger had waned and indeed, he had attempted, in that inimitable style of his, to shy people away from the head-to-head.

Maybe he liked it? a chef commented to me as we peeled onions in tandem.

Don't be a fuckface, I reprimanded him as we both began to cry.

Some of 'em do, that's all I'm saying, he gushed.

Yeah, well not Billy, I replied adamantly as I wiped yet more onion juice into my already swollen eyes.

Has he ever offered to dog your doodle? my compatriot enquired, his face now puffed and bloated.

What are you, some kind of fucking jailhouse shrink?

Maybe it's you that likes to dog fucking doodles, huh?

Fuck you, shit for brains.

Yeah, fuck you too – you little queer crybaby.

This is the kind of compassion you are shown in the big

kitchen, even from your own countrymen, many of whom do not have the brains they first developed in the womb. Billy a bandit? No, I seriously doubted it, and besides that, I have always been an exponent of the art of character judging; I can do it instantly, which is why I still have my good looks and the use of most of my faculties. I have not arrived at the station I am on today by allowing people to pull the wool over my eyes. On top of that I had lived with the guy twenty-four-seven for a year or more and when you are bunked together for that period of time there are not many secrets that can be withheld. It is the same in the joint, after a three-month stretch you know whether or not you can trust your jailbird buddy to look after your back – the front can take care of itself, thanks.

I thought about taking a meat hammer to the goon who had just insulted my soul brother, maybe rough the cretin up a bit in the dry store just to keep my hand in. I have always been a brawler, but was never one for the long haul. I prefer the element of surprise and to accomplish the task in the quickest possible time; at school they fondly used to call me the shit-house assassin. That was where I did my best work. I am not one to be bare-knuckle brawling while a throbbing mob of my peers stand around and bait the contestants. No indeed, in such matters it is prudent to strike first, and to strike hard, after this you can rest safely in the knowledge that the next time a question arises whereby some fool feels the need to humiliate you or a comrade, he might pause to recollect what happened to the last gook who tried it. This is called prevention and, as any good doctor will tell you, it is better than cure.

Slurs like these are a matter of honour. Not only is the afflicted person your roommate, but he is a chef too, a member of the brotherhood. Back in those days kitchens still had unwritten mantras, manly shit like 'honour' and 'one for all'.

Men in the kitchen are never prepared to turn the other cheek, and that is why the plan went ahead for good or worse.

I feel fooking sick, Billy told me, as we got ready for the dirty work ahead.

Well, you should of thought of that, huh?

Despite what you might think, it is not straightforward to grab a cocktail barman, blindfold him and bundle him up to a TV lounge on the sixth floor. Such ploys take a lot of planning and everyone has to play their part; management have to be diverted, the porters need bribing, and other non-associated live-in staff have to be kept in the dark like champignons. These events rarely go off without a hitch, especially elevator rides when there are a dozen of you holding onto a wriggling bundle. There is always an old lady who cannot sleep, a hooker coming or going, a businessman with time on his hands, or a connoisseur in search of a late night cognac and maybe more. Hotels rarely sleep, they are merely rooming houses for the unstable and the restless and as such there is no such thing as privacy. Having said all of that, fate was on our side, as it sometimes is with the righteous.

Up in the TV lounge we unwrapped our victim and subdued his temper while a few others barricaded the door. It could be a long night and just in case we had come prepared. It's the thrill, of course, that drives; good common sense and rationality never barge in on such circumstances and the reckless always lead the way. And this was exactly what had occurred, we had our perp – as they say stateside – and now all we had to do was make him squeal, but how? Luckily the sous had brought a pair of fish scissors; he hadn't climbed that far up the ladder by not being able to think ahead.

The same could not be said of the rest of us, however. They

say that evil thrives when good men do nothing, well we were a few good men and we were taking matters into our own hands. There ought to be more of it. No sooner had we uncovered our prey than he began lashing out in all directions – he wasn't a small man either, although those can often be the worst. His antics came as a complete surprise, as unexpected as receiving a Christmas bonus. A few people copped direct hits and for a few minutes there was panic, a half dozen well-intentioned chefs caught like rabbits in the headlights. Finally however the guy ran out of puff, it is a phenomenon you can see any Friday night behind pubs, the man who shoots off his best shots first and fails to strike a decisive blow will usually end up losing the bout. After those initial exertions, when it was clear that his ploy had failed, he broke down and wept. Remorse always follows aggression just as sure as a hangover follows a night on the tiles. We had seen off the worst of it now and all that was left was not to fall for such a lily-livered play.

Interrogation followed and, as per usual, there were too many chiefs and not enough injuns. Finally after several hours the guy confessed to it all in a round-about fashion; he was being blackmailed by the panty-wearing fiend who had escaped that sorry night, he had fallen in with lustful and bizarre people with so many fetishes that they made Leopold von Sacher-Masoch and his cronies look like the Pilgrim Fathers. He was into these perverts big time, having first run foul of them in the annual stud poker tournament, and after that not even his tips would cover the interest. He was living hand to mouth, in their mouths and their hands, and if only he could procure them a well-built kind of boy to fool around with, he could be free of their dirty clutches.

I think Billy was kind of flattered by the idea that the barman had decided upon him as a worthy candidate. He was sorry now anyhow, that shithead creeping Jesus of a bar boy, sorry that he'd been stupid enough to think that such a wild notion might actually bear fruit, that he could just substitute a first-year apprentice chef for his own unworthy self – but he was tired of it all. He had no money to flee abroad and no one to confide in, he couldn't go to the police because they knew his kind and were never in any hurry to assist such people with their sordid implications. When a few of us nodded sympathetically, the tide was beginning to turn the fool's way and he knew it. He went for the kill, about as messily as a Newfoundland seal clubber. If only we could help him out he'd be gone from our lives by the week's end, all he needed was a little stash to enable him to reach Gibraltar, he had relatives there who ran a sleazy bar and were making big dough from the British navy and various actors while they waited to resume filming in Spain.

Funnily enough, it all sounded quite logical, and that is the way these kinds of messes often flatten out in the big hotel, for despite our personal acrimonies and tensions, we are all children of the night. The sous ordered a whip round, it wasn't much, but it was enough to see the guy to the ferry terminal, after that he would have to hustle his way.

Drinks were produced by us and cocktail cherries by the barman, and we toasted our success. Like all good chefs we had used good practical sense with a dollop of hot-headedness and as per usual we had come up smelling like swine. The barman kept his word and left that following Friday. There were still people who thought that Billy was suspect – little did they or he know however, that within a few short weeks an opportunity for redemption would present itself – and as ever, Billy would fail miserably to live up to expectations. He was always a man short somehow.

I got called to F&B after Billy had gone to find out whether or not he'd passed his first-year cookery certificate (and he had, but only just). I had my own seat in there, just like outside the headmaster's office at school. I passed with a credit – how, I'm not sure, it must have been my charm. But those creeps weren't finished with me, not by a long stretch of the neck.

Now then Luiz, one began, all this stuff about fatherhood that's . . .

Fatherhood? No fucking way man, I replied angrily.

Look, calm down, you're too good a chef to lose, all we need to hear is your version, that's all, okay?

So I told them about the tramp and her twin, and for the love of St Patrick it was the most blasphemous blarney of all times, but – they bought it. Phew! I whistled as I strode back to the arena, life was getting way too hot to handle around here: crazy broads with hidden agendas; Billy with his pinball addiction; and the Duce – what the fuck's up with him? It was all crowding in on me, and I am not the kind to be fettered. Maybe I'd just go AWOL?

25.

Killer Queen

I am a good judge of character and I knew there was something queer about Bumble right from the off. I remember saying to Billy, there's something fucking odd about that Bumble. But Billy, he was not one to see the obvious. One afternoon he returned to our hovel all red and breathless, trembling far more than usual.

What now? I asked him, having presumed, foolishly, that in Billy's case there couldn't be yet another odd saga for him to stumble arse over tit into. I was wrong; yet again the curse of Billy's naiveté had struck. He had accepted an invite from a renowned vamp of a waiter to share an afternoon sauna. I mean, why? After I had calmed him down he told me he'd just been offered fifty quid to give said waiter a quick blow job.

Fifty quid! I whistled, did he want swallowing or not?

Fooking hell no! he cried.

What? You did and he didn't want it swallowed? Or you didn't because he wanted it gulped down?

You fooking animal, I didn't do either, I'm no faggot.

He wasn't, but still, fifty nicker is fifty nicker, three weeks' apprentice chef's wages, and a quick blow job doesn't seem such hard work to earn that kind of bread, unless you have to swallow the load too, then it's a matter for negotiation. These incidents aren't unusual in the confines of the hotel; folks become bored, and try endless ways to inject interest into their between-shift lives. Management turns a blind eye, what keeps a team happy is good for productivity I suppose.

Not long after Billy left, the above-mentioned waiter tried the same ruse with me, although his version of the account was that Billy had gladly done it for forty. That was when I hit the bastard with my steel; these perverts will try anything to get another set of gums around their tackle. Anyhow, let me assure you that Billy was never that kind of boy, no indeed, but there are boys who are that kind inside of the walls, and one of those boys was Bumble.

Bumble had pot-holed skin, lank brown hair and the torso of a cadaver. He got himself into one hell of a mess, and he almost managed to take the rest of us down with him. It all started when word spread that a few of the live-in girls had begun to complain about their underwear vanishing from staff bathrooms. This is not an odd occurrence, there are many men who rather enjoy the sensuous feel of women's lingerie, but who are either too tight or too afraid to purchase it for themselves – there is only so many times you can pull off the old birthday present trick. What began as a trickle – a bra here, a pair of panties there, the odd slip or nightie – turned into a rather disturbing avalanche, and soon everyone became a suspect and consequently a matter for debate. At chow times the girls somewhat revelled in questioning their choices for suspects in the public domain, and no matter whether you were innocent, somehow you felt guilty, stained by shame as they say in the laundry.

In the kitchen, people began to look at each other suspiciously; the section chefs began a systematic purge on suspected cross-dressers by dragging them down to the larder and forcibly inspecting their preference in underwear. Some became tainted by it all, and as the pressure built no one escaped the innuendo or anger. Observation and surveillance parties were organized and the girls stopped drying their smalls in the bathrooms, and, mercifully, the incidences dropped off.

However, complacency has a way of gaining a foothold, especially in staff quarters, and a few weeks later the affair flared up again. In these kinds of situations you cannot casually sit back and allow events to run their natural course, to wait for the thief to slip up as they say in the apparel industry, no indeed, more proactive intervention is required and so it turned out.

A week later we were on shift, mindlessly hacking up old meat for a staff pie, when several managers descended on the kitchen like census takers. One by one we were led off to a back office while a bevy of girls booed and hissed. Inside the room were two police officers who took our names and then, accompanied by management, searched our rooms.

This is a bad kind of scene, good underwear isn't cheap, and it somewhat soured me toward the whole live-in thing. I mean, it was okay them looking for contraband satin, but what if they uncovered other incriminating shit in the process, how did we stand then? I had no time to ring the family solicitor though, because he was in Nassau sunbathing on the old man's tab. They are never available when you need them, have you noticed that?

To be fair we had been offered the choice; to assist voluntarily, or have it done by legal means, but if you opted for the latter course, it sure as hell made you look stone-cold guilty. So off I went, I had nothing untoward to conceal, Billy neither. After my flings with the law, I had remained of good character. But no sooner had the old Bill ransacked mine and

Billy's few possessions, than we were escorted back to the kitchen feeling like common criminals.

I bet it was you, wasn't it? a chef tried to rile me, but I just laughed the innuendo off.

How could it be? Your missus is my alibi! I teased him.

Some did get caught out, however. There are more cross-dressers in hotels than you may realize, and many people had some explaining to do. The big haul, however, still hadn't been uncovered, and the place was buzzing like a swarm of angry bees.

Which is about the point where Bumble comes into the equation.

I should have known it would be a chef, although I would have lain off my bets heavily in favour of a pastry geek. But no, it turned out to be the larder section and the fish section that were smeared by Bumble's fetishes.

When they searched Bumble's room, even the police were amazed. The guy had panties and bras stuffed everywhere. The final tally proved to be upward of four hundred items of intimate apparel – and not all from the hotel, either. The police had hit the jackpot with Bumble and the recent wave of mysterious undergarment disappearances from clotheslines around town had been solved in one fell swoop.

The shit hit the fan big time, through Bumble's inability to control his deviancy we had all been yanked into the bright glare of the fetish spotlight.

Bumble eh? a porter asked me as we sat opposite one another eating breakfast.

Keep your fucking voice down, I whispered angrily.

Why?

Why, you fool? Because if you so much as mention that

pervert in here with all those girls on that table over there, they'll rip us to shreds. Don't you see that we're all guilty?

Guilty of fucking what? I don't steal panties and jack-off in them, do you?

That was beside the point, I told him quietly, and it was too, there but for the grace of God et cetera, and it could quite easily have been me, had I not been more circumspect. But that is another story.

Bumble vanished for a few weeks, some said to attend therapy in Amsterdam. It was a messy business. We saw him again a month later when he arrived to collect his few remaining possessions and outstanding pay. He was dressed in a rather flattering summer frock, one that billowed out seductively when he walked his newly acquired feminine strut. It was quite erotic, especially when the harsh lighting silhouetted his curvaceous body – anyhow, he was wearing these ankle-strap sandals that accentuated the definition of his highly waxed legs, a large straw hat that hid his growing hair and Sandy Shaw-style sunglasses.

Shit, is that that pervert Bumble? one of the line asked another.

Got himself some real hard she-bitch therapy, another answered.

Fucking Jesus, I'd do that man, wouldn't you?

You'd better fucking believe it bud, any which way it came.

Chefs have short memories and uncontrollable urges. Bumble on the other hand was no longer a chef, Bumble was one of the beautiful people and much in demand on the working-girl scene. Men are queer in that kind of way, and, as we are oft to say on the griddle, a faint heart never won a fair hand.

The Bumble incident unsettled me. Not because he'd been pinching panties, he could keep that gig, more because he'd had the brazen gall to return to the scene of his many crimes in his true persona. There's a lot to be said for it, honesty, and to be honest, it's one of the virtues you rarely see among the milieu of hotel staff. It made me appreciate, if I hadn't before, that all of us were hiding something within those walls.

26.

Everybody Was Kung Fu Fighting

After that, it was Billy who again stepped up to bat in the hope of swinging a giant home run, not for womanhood you understand, but for the boys. New blood had arrived. How fucking weird is it to see two kids looking as gormless as you had eighteen months ago on your first day in the brave new world? Did I feel sorry for them? Not one bit of it; I only hoped that these poor bastards got it as hard as we'd had it, and then some more just for good measure. It's great to see the brigade's reaction when you are on the other side of the fence, to hear their thoughts and watch their faces when they first set eyes on fresh meat. And this time they really did have something to feast upon. Fucking hell, if it ain't Fu Man fucking Chu! That was how they reacted when they first saw Wong; there were other jibes, of course, only I don't intend to write them here as I am no xenophobe.

I was right at the birth of East meets West, I suppose, and I never realized it, right there at the pivotal point when Fusion commenced. What a turn up for the books then, either the brigade was going to have the proverbial field day, or Wong would stand his ground. Unfortunately for us, everyone was Kung Fu fighting.

These puerile jousts and silly games that chefs indulge in are nothing more than rights of passage, indoctrination into the hothouse, things that generations before have gone through. These two new kids on the block, however, weren't quite ready to partake of jovial pranks, for both were highly unsuited for a professional kitchen – it was a bad year to recruit apprentices, or so an F&B told us completely off the record, it was either these two or nothing.

K was a gangly kid with rampant acne and the kind of coordination that you see in newborn giraffes. Besides that, he was already far too tall to make it as a chef. If you study kitchens you will see that almost to a man there is a uniform code of height tolerance; once you start to climb over, say, five six, then the job becomes difficult. Kitchen benches are the bane of your life, like rocks are to washerwomen; you are always bent over one and when you are not bent over a benchtop you are scrunched over a flattop. The lower your centre of gravity, the better you will succeed in the kitchen, for chefs are sturdy robust beings with short legs and long arms. Put a toque on a five-ten kid and he will never stand a hope of making it to the line simply because he will be forever picking up his hat after he's caught it on the extractor canopies. Tall gangly kids who are all flaying arms and legs are a real menace in a busy kitchen, they demand more width to turn than there is available and they cannot navigate the steep steps many kitchens are strewn with.

Don't give that fucker my prep to take downstairs okay? the saucier told me. He looks like fucking Bambi and I don't want to have to re-prep every day, you understand?

Of course I understood, a kid as ungainly as that could drop a whole morning's prep while in the windmill action of trying to grab his hat again. That's how K came to be known as Bambi. It wasn't the most flattering pet name I suppose, but it was better than Don Quixote, which was the other fancied option.

As for Wong, well he never got rid of the handle Chu – sometimes the mud sticks as soon as it hits. As a whole the brigade wasn't at all happy with the year's new signings, there was much consternation and muttering and no one wanted to be the first to have a go with one of those goons – so off to the pot wash they went.

Around mid morning on most mornings I would make it my business to go downstairs, for I had a vested interest in continuing my fine rapport with the KPs and they in turn were always happy to see my smiling face. There was no harmony down in the slophouse, however, not like there had been during my and Billy's tenure. The KPs were fed up with the backchat from the new brats and the attitude of modern kids was grating on them.

It ain't like it used to be, they told me disconsolately while they raced cockroaches, these kids can't even mop a fucking floor properly, what chance has a kid got if he can't handle a mop 'n' bucket, huh? I nodded sympathetically; the whole world was going to shit and no one seemed that bothered.

The trouble started over something trivial. It always does – look at Custer.

Billy was having one of his bad days and I think Bumble's break for freedom had unsettled him. He kept on about the damned affair for several weeks afterwards and in a kitchen this is not good practice. Sauciers and fish chefs do not like to be constantly harangued about what it would feel like to grow breasts or even bitch tits. These men have enough on their plate day in and day out and most of them were sick of Billy's continual exploration of gender reassignment procedures. And then K and Chu re-emerged in the cauldron all wrinkled fingers and bloodshot eyes. Now Chu, he was what you might call a know-it-all, you couldn't teach the kid anything because as soon as you commenced on the subject matter at hand the kid would be contradicting you. Christ Almighty, this is not the kind of attitude that chefs want and before the week was out Chu found himself in everyone's bad books – especially Billy's, for Billy didn't take at all to a wet pup giving him grief over the simplest of chores. They fell out in a bad way over the weekly cleaning of the stock vats, three huge pots with hinged lids and taps on the base that we used to make up stocks and consommés. They had been cleaning these out, or at least Chu was supposed to be cleaning them under Billy's tuition. In the middle of the job they somehow managed to come to blows and a veg chef stepped into the fray, not necessarily to stop them, but to tell them to get the fuck away from his courgette Provencale. It might have been stopped there, nipped in the bud as florists say after dirty weekends, but in a kitchen such spontaneous interruptions to the daily routine are often aided and abetted for distraction, and so some fool can run a book.

Within a week the place was like Caesar's Palace as people scrambled to bet money they didn't even have. Honour reared its ugly head again, like a tramp waking up after the mother of all meth sessions, and before Billy knew it, he was duty bound to engage in a few rounds of fisticuffs to teach the kid a lesson. Fighting wasn't his bag, but as is the wont of men with time on their hands and no money to drink away, he was left with no choice – the TKO wasn't on offer, and nor was the dive: Don King wasn't involved. I told him that he'd gotten himself in way too deep, that I thought the kid Chu could handle himself a bit; he looked a bit tasty, as the East Enders say.

Chu was laying off good bets around the place based on the fact he was always demonstrating his Kung Fu skills – he was a black belt apparently, and an ex junior kickboxing champion in Mandalay. Two people were chosen to stand corners, and when that happens things are getting very serious indeed. Billy's man was called Jimmy and he was a demi-chef, one of those guys bright enough to get through catering school but with not an ounce of self-motivation, destined always to live in the limbo land of the halfway house. He was a decent enough guy, though, and he took to training Billy with a passion. Jimmy had been a bantamweight in his sparring days back in the hood, and he and Billy went off every afternoon running along the beach, shadow boxing in the TV lounge and skipping in the ballroom. It was all very professional, what with the towels, the Vaseline, the bandages, the punching sides of beef in the coolroom – the whole Rocky Balboa thing.

Still, it is making me edgy, I told Billy, why not just get a monkey wrench from Danny over in maintenance and lobotomize the fucker, presto, problem solved.

Nah, Billy told me indignantly, boxing is the sport of fooking gentlemen, ain't you ever heard of Queensbury rules?

Sure, I told him, that means you can't bite, kidney punch or sneak in a blow below the belt – why don't you two just go for handbags at dawn and be fucking done with it? The Marquess of Queensbury wasn't big on fun, that's how wrestling evolved.

The date was set, it was to be an outdoor event, and Billy's luck continued to run foul of Lady Fortune. It ain't easy to dance on shingle, to outrun your opponent so to speak, and Billy would get weighed down in the sand. The odds shifted dramatically. They set the date for my day off and because I had already pre-arranged a trip home I decided to give the fight of the century a miss – who needed it? That spooked Billy too, he was glum over the fact that he wouldn't have my moral support when it mattered. The odds blew out too far to be reconciled, it was a one-man show, odds on, all monies, no more bets being taken, the fix was in.

I went home, but I spent a restless weekend thinking about the situation my mucker had again got himself into. Had it gone the distance or had the towel been thrown in? Had it been broken up before it even began by a holidaying JP? Had a blow even been struck or had they just danced about like a couple of fairies high on wine gums? All would be revealed, I guessed – it normally was.

I caught the late train back.

Five fucking quid down the drain, moaned Harry the night porter, as he let me in the servant's entrance. I feared the worst, but it was worse than that.

They did it, then? I asked.

Oh yeah, Harry said gloomily, but it weren't exactly what you'd call a spectacle. Twenty-three seconds the sous told me, that's how long it had lasted.

Billy had taken up the Queensbury pose and Chu had taken up the kung fu stance and then Whammo! Two quick kicks to the chops and it was all over red rover. Now Billy was on sick leave, three teeth gone, one cut lip and a broken nose, and he looked a fucking mess.

Of course, the sous said, it's all up to you now.

Me?

Well, he's your boy.

He ain't my fucking boy!

Still the same thing, it's your year – that Fu Man Chu'll be all over you like Bruce Lee.

It's nothing to do with me.

Suit yourself, the sous shrugged, they got a book going on it already.

Fuck 'em all. It ain't my beef.

It's all to do with sweet natural justice kid, like; you gotta teach that kung fu fighting fuckhead a hard lesson.

Yeah well, ain't it queer how those two tramps, justice and revenge, always end up in bed together having a gal-on-gal wrestle? Shit yeah, there ain't no thing as moral justice, no such thing as account settled – the fucking tab's always running, and the book's always open, one day you're the fucking champion and the next you're little more than a fast-talking challenger with small balls and big ambitions.

Billy came back to work an even paler shadow of himself, and Chu strutted around like a cock in a henhouse. The section chefs kept nagging me, Chu kept glaring at me from his bench while he peeled blanched tomatoes. The pressure built, and then it reached cracking point.

Right! I said, whipping off my apron, discarding my hat and downing the wooden spoon, the corn fritter batter can fucking wait.

Chu had slunk out back for a smoke. I headed downstairs and found the KPs. Cut me a length of that hose there, I told them snappily.

Aye boss, they responded pronto, trouble at mill?

Shorter, yeah, that's great. I climbed back up into the main kitchen, my sap on the rise, strode outside straight past the Duce's office and averted my gaze from his quizzical stare. Chu turned and looked at me cockily.

Hel –, he started. WHACK! The kid went down like a sack of bean sprouts, but then bounced back up as quick as rice in a paddy field, taking the stance, a big red welt blooming on his cheek.

More? I asked him.

You ain't got the balls! he chided me.

I smiled, took a step forward and as he began to make his golden slipper move I kicked him in the gooleys, and with clogs on that's no mean feat. This time there was no second coming; he was rolling around like a dog with a rattrap on its nuts.

One more word out of you kung fu boy, and next time it'll be you that's taking a free trip down to casualty, okay?

It all ended there, out by the bins. How very apt.

27.

20th Century Boy

Perhaps it is now pertinent that we study the duties of the head chef, for theirs is a life that all we underlings aspire to, but very few ever achieve. The reason for this is quite simple: attrition.

The drop-out rate amongst apprentice chefs is alarmingly high, so is the rate for those who have actually completed indentures and then come to their senses and flee. The body can survive because it can tend itself; the mind however is far more susceptible to disease. Your cuts, burns, scalds, aches and pains will eventually heal, but the psychological damage inflicted by stress, demands, immense concentration, anger, paranoia and fear, will most likely stay with you forever. Even these days, after having been out of a kitchen for almost six years, I am still prone to outbursts of temper for no logical reason, moments when I feel the need to strangle someone just for the sheer hell of it. I am still hounded by stress, still stalked by paranoia, not to mention several ex-waitresses waving paternity results. And, of course, I'm still acutely aware of how badly damaged I became during my twenty-year stint on the ranges, the last eight or so of these suffered as head chef in varying sizes of establishment in different parts of the world. I made it, yeah, I made it to Duce myself, and I fought every inch of the way to get there, and when I did, my workload and the stress associated with it quadrupled, just like the paternity claims.

There wasn't anyone to blame or anyone to turn to, all there was, was me. Me and a brigade depending on me to do everything for them other than wipe their goddamned arses, and sometimes, I guess, they even needed that. In the top job you get pressured from both sides, squeezed like an orange in a juice press. On the one side, management is forever niggling you about discipline, about leading by example, about fucking swearing all the time, about press releases, about new hours, about training, about hiring, about firing, about every goddamned thing other than the *quality* of the food you're striving to produce.

And then the brigade puts the squeeze on you: why can't we have this piece of equipment, extra hands, an agreed cut-off time for latecomers, more booze, better pay, better meat, regular fucking days off, holidays at a normal time of the goddamned year, better waiters, cheap waitresses, carte blanche, our whites laundered and our feet rubbed? Jesus H. fucking Christ. I spent every day caught between the crosshairs of these two warring factions like a UN ambassador, constantly striving to appease one group or another: always negotiating, molly coddling, supporting, sympathizing, explaining, rationalizing, mitigating, agreeing, disagreeing, in one door and out of the other and in-between all of that I tried to source food, write menus, teach the brigade how to prepare and cook it to my style and the wait staff how to sell and serve it.

The brigade arrives late and leaves early, their job done, while on most days the poor fucker at the top, the Duce, works a hundred hours plus per week and then some. It never stops: the phone, the orders, the suppliers, the cry babies, the axe wielders, the bean counters, the owners, the diners, the cleaners, the delivery guys, the pregnant, the menopausal, the ill, the desperate and the suicidal. You are at the beck and call of each and every one of these people; it is your shoulder they cry on and your ear they whinge into. At the bottom, there is no one you can trust, and life is exactly the same at the top. Oh I know they crap on about best buddy sous chefs, but that's a crock. There's no sous who isn't looking for the top job whether the Duce is a life-long pal or not. All of those pig-dogs will seize the earliest opportunity to pull the welcome mat out of your office, and brother, if you aren't savvy enough to see the glint off that blade they're carrying, then the next time you see it will be after they're yanking it out from between your shoulder blades. As the Duce you are all things to all people, Mother Superior and Father Confessor all rolled into one fluffy bundle of white.

The Duce's day starts early, in fact, it starts the very moment he regains consciousness in the still twilight hours in some bed his spine isn't accustomed to; already his mind is humming, pinning up mental post-it notes all over the show. What did we run out of last night? What meez do I need? Did I take that fucking osso out of hibernation? Why did I roster the pastry geek off today of all fucking days? This unconscious stream of thought continues while the Duce goes through a carefully trimmed and expedient personal hygiene routine. He is in the kitchen an hour, sometimes two, before the brigade. He might get paid for that time although it is highly unlikely – in today's stringently controlled budget-aware kitchen, the Duce is expected to make it all run like clockwork, but not like *A Clockwork Orange*.

After thirty minutes of calls, arguments, debates about last night's service, your attitude, and brainless wait staff, it is time to yank open the coolroom door. Shit that was bunged into the coolroom the night before slides out onto the floor. There is plum sauce all over a badly covered tray of fish, pieces of turned vegetable and al fucking falfa in almost everything. Piece by piece he begins hauling it all out; as ever there is a large pot strategically placed into which yesterday's soup, several old sauces, limp vegetables and other assorted debris can be flung, and then disguised with curry powder to create today's potage. All the trays will need changing, all of the cling too. Then the floor will need sweeping and all this before the first of the day's deliveries begin appearing; if you don't see the coolroom floor before this daily ritual occurs, you are fucked. After this the sinks look as if you've already served a hundred covers, there are pots, tubs, trays, and pans stretching back like a traffic jam on a foggy morning. In-between all of this activity the phone continues to ring and various heads from other departments wander in and out taking the time to rag your arse over some petty indiscretion committed by one of your troops. By the time the first of the brigade arrives, bleary-eyed, hungover, still stoned and with the first signs of malaria, you have already re-written their job lists and made notes on the condition of their section or meez trolley. That's when the bitching starts. How comes I'm on fucking pastry? Four fucking late orders again last night. Why can't those shitheads stop taking my garnishes? Can you tell them to make their own garnishes chef? Ah, Jesus fucking H. Osso? Man I ain't got the time to do osso, you seen my fucking prep list? Say we don't get the sea trout, are we just using John West at lunch then?

What? No one told me there was a table of thirty for lunch. Bring me the dickhead who took the booking, or his head if we still need his body. NOW! Shit everywhere, prep still not done, no fucking fish order again, the duty manager wants a chicken caesar salad for lunch even though it's off the menu now, there's still a table of four sitting in the bar, chef, is it okay if they wait for their grandmother? Fucking hell no, tell one of those idiots to get their butt in here and order pronto. Clean down, only three and a half hours until the dinner service, drive home with a head full of worries. Drink two cans of beer, watch daytime soaps, use your own phone to chase up the fish guy.

Back two hours later, the fish has been dumped and not even refrigerated; those bastards are going to cop it hard tomorrow morning. That late table of four wasn't at all happy with being rushed, what's the problem? There's no sour bread, no sea trout, no tarragon, you still have an hour to find alternatives. Big lull, spend the first hour unsure as to whether to start tomorrow's prep or hang tight for the inevitable fall out, and no sooner do you tell the team to start prepping for tomorrow than a waiter appears clutching twelve dockets.

It's a madhouse out there, chief! he yaps gleefully, it's gonna be a big one tonight!

Well that's just fucking swell, I can hardly wait. The waiter is back into the fray, his pencil sharpened and his mind empty. Get fucking ready, I tell the line, make sure you've got enough tempura? And then BANG! You can't remember anything for an hour, two, three. Everything around you is a blurry funk, and by the time the rush has all but abated you notice that you have a couple of decent burns, a nick on the knuckles from reaching into the oven bare-handed to retrieve wraps, and one mother of a headache. All that remains is to get the place straight again, and as you deliver instructions there are problems with desserts and requests from six or seven tables to join them for a drink. On the drive home you are sucking most of the grime and goo out from beneath your fingernails. What about duck tomorrow? Maybe poussin? Where can I find a competent baker? The steamer needs a clean down and we need the mandolin sharpened or replaced, and why are there never any fucking Band Aids?

A long time ago I used to think that all the Duce did was sit in his office and write menus, read porno mags and drink for free at the bar. It was the kind of gig that I quite fancied, but like all apprentices, I was too fucking stupid to see the plain truth. Service after service I hankered for those good old days, days of irresponsibility, binge drinking and comradeship. It's fucking lonely at the top.

One day, when you are the Duce, a sprightly girl from reception will bound into your office, ponytail swinging and arse pumping, and she'll dump onto your already cluttered desk a stack of CVs, maybe her phone number too. It's time to hire a new apprentice, ruin some bastard's life forever. It gets you thinking back to your own time, mulling over bad decisions. You start to wonder where all the good men went. And not only that, but why is that come hiring time all of those sons and daughters whose G&T-sloshing mothers had once cooed in your ear about just how desperate Donny or Donna was to be a chef, are nowhere to be found?

Hesitantly you pick up the CV sitting atop the pile; this dude has a Bachelor of Arts in tourism and a Masters in nutritional sciences, you plop it straight into the bin. There is no berth in the bunkhouse for a know-it-all with more paperwork than Frank Abagnale. The next jarhead has an angelic-looking face and lists his hobbies as netball and macramé; Jesus fucking H. a kid like that will be ripped to shreds within a week, plop, into the bin funny buddy. They are a sorry-looking bunch, the offspring of parents with no idea just what their progeny are applying for. Plop, plop, plop, three more get the bullet in quick succession. Now, here's a girl who looks too damned free and easy to be hanging around a professional kitchen, a girl like this will be up the duff within a year and you will be back to square one, plop. You are left with six or seven, maybe ten, and before you study their ambitions you study their faces. Which one of these kids would look good in a police photograph? Okay, now you are down to the knob as we say in the trade, right at the bottom of the barrel and from this juncture there is no point in hoping for miracles.

Whoever the final choice is, it will take three or four years of your life, infinite patience, frustration, exasperation and regrets. The chances are that no matter whom you choose, within a year they will have realized that the whole job is a mug's game and they will be off. Still, there is always hope, and on the interview day you let them do the talking – if they can't talk or are too shy, then mentally you eliminate them, likewise the kid who won't fucking shut up. Somewhere in-between there has to be a kid who can orate, but knows when to keep his or her fucking mouth shut too. That's the kid I'm after, the kid who has a nervous confidence and eyes on him like coal embers. Hopefully I'll get him, and if I do I'll make that little son of a bitch the kitchen pussy for a year and after that I'll turn the fucker loose on the line, then he'll be hooked and there'll be no turning back . . . I'll have successfully created another monster, an exact caricature of me, and that kid will walk, talk, eat, shit and drink, just like me. He will be my boy, or she will be my girl, whatever I say will go, no matter how fucking bizarre that request might appear to the outside world. Forget the outside world, it no longer exists!

I can teach you about everything you need to know: cookery, life, sex, drugs and drinking, just sign right here sweetmeat, and if you can't sign your own name, all the fucking better, just put your mark right there shit for brains … and say, has anyone ever told you what nice lips you've got?

28.

Waterloo

I'm always asked about the advent of women in the brigade, has it made big kitchens pussy whipped? Personally I don't mind, it gave me more scope to operate that's for sure, but to some, when the fairer sex began to flood in, the whole nature of the Job changed. It is much like an ex-bachelor coming home to find hair in the sink, pink Snoopy cushions on the sofa and chintz curtains where before there was beer, TV and old yellowed newspaper. Women changed the very infrastructure and ecosystem of the kitchen, they rubbed off the sharp abrasive edges with their feminine curves and brought with them a whole host of problems that up until then no one had had to bother about – like lavatorial cleanliness.

Now, why is it that as soon as the first girl came into a kitchen, management decided that it was okay for her to use guest toilets? What's wrong with the shithouse? Sure it's in a pretty bad state, all chefs suffer from perpetual intestinal problems acquired through eating irregularly and drinking too much, and okay there's pretty crude graffiti on the door back, but, you know, if it's good enough for us, eh? Maybe there wasn't a sanitary product disposal bin, but as far as I know those things aren't too expensive. Why is it that it's apparently fine for a male brigade to make do and mend, but if it's a mixed brigade more attention is paid to the little things? Like, do we really need tissues and air fresheners in commercial kitchens when we've needed a new blender for the past year? Do we tolerate the allowances made for female brigade members while the guys are horse-whipped over the smallest indiscretion? These were the kinds of issues that began to come up. Perhaps it's just the whole change ethos; everyone was happy with the way things were.

No sooner did we have women in the big kitchen than we had to deal with maternity leave, crèches, menstrual cycles, depression, yo-yo dieting, hair nets, body hygiene, obscenity, obesity (Hey chef can we get some detour signs for that lard ass in the pastry? Yesterday I caught that mother sucking cream straight outta the piping bag!), and a myriad of other problems that all made the job harder than it already was. Where a sliver of soap and a grubby pox-infested handtowel had sufficed for a hundred years, all of a sudden we had to have liquid soap dispensers and hand dryers. The first woman in whites I saw was a feisty young lass from North London. The first day she was in the kitchen they put her in charge of cleaning the fryers and that is a godawful job. It is stinky, fatty, hard labour draining the old fat while constantly unblocking the drain-plug caked with the detritus of fifty hard services, leaning right in and shovelling up the crud, scrubbing the fryers, washing the baskets, and finally re-filling the mothers. The girl couldn't lift either the drums full of waste oil or the new blocks of lard. This was not her fault – there were quite a few pastry chefs who wouldn't have been able to do it either – but, the point was that if the girl couldn't physically do that part of the job, then feasibly she couldn't be put on roster *to* do it? This led to resentment; it was early days and chefs weren't at all happy that a person could be excused some shit job due to physical weakness.

Where is the line? What do you do when the line is crossed? Is it okay for the male brigade to continue to act like the deviant barbarians they are when there is a member of the gentler sex in their midst? Is it still okay to grab each other's undercarriage just for fun, or is that now a dismissible offence? Is it still acceptable to talk rather openly about the merits, both physical and mental, of a particular waitress or waiter, while a girl is within earshot? And just what do you call the buggers? A kitchen doesn't use names, it uses terms of endearment: spud, big bollocks, curly, hell man, fuckface, bitch, bastard, shit for brains, dog breath, Cyclops, muffin, Brutus, to name but a few of the nicer ones that come to mind. Certainly it isn't okay to address a female colleague as luv, darling, honey, sweetmeat, lamb chop, saddle-bags, et cetera, so all you are left with is the name, I guess, and how boring is that? Say, Susan, pass me the bech please, doesn't have anywhere near the same kind of ring as, Say, Butt Face, sling me the bech, huh, and quick about it!

These were interesting developments and it took many people a long time to come to grips with them, like it does apprentice chefs with women's breasts. In cookery, at least, I would say that the majority of women who did, and still, come into the Game, have assimilated well. They have evolved to be just as competitive, just as skilled, and just as mouthy as your average male chef. And good on them for that, it was, after all, a testosterone fortress and the first, as is often the case, definitely had it the worst.

These days it is all taken for granted and that is how it should be, apart from the boghouse thing – women still seem to get a higher standard of shithouse, and why is that? And finally there was always the worry, and there still is I guess, of the curse of the sweethearts.

It takes a fair while to get a chef into the groove of a particular place, for the brigade to respect and trust him, or her, and when it was all boys it was a good investment. Sure a couple of pastry chefs would run off to Geneva now and again but on the whole no one minded putting in the hard yards. They are more sceptical now, however, for the most despised crime is that of your fish chef and your new pastry girl eloping to Vegas one night. Many good men have already been lost this way, good women too I suppose, although experience has taught me that it is the men who are always the keenest to abscond – perhaps because they cannot trust their true love around so much rampant chauvinism? Women though brought love and peace, and many men were keen to embrace that new philosophy, if only for a night.

29.

Farewell

If you think catering is an industry where you will earn the big bucks – then, friend, you are an imbecile, and as such you get everything you deserve.

What you earn for what you put in has always been dramatically out of kilter in the business of hospitality. They have figured it all out over a very long period of time and have neither the inclination nor need to alter the status quo in favour of the Worker. The long-established tradition has been to employ the unstable and the disadvantaged; there is nothing new about the philosophy, it has been en vogue since Gus first grabbed up soot-covered kids from London streets and gave them something to aim for – an early death. This modern trend toward the intake of diploma-holding swats and well-groomed over-educated types has only made the industry top heavy; like every other profession today, the worldwide hospitality industry is over-managed and under-staffed. The grunts (the obnoxious sweating pig on the chargrill or the foul-mouthed bitch on the veg) are doing all the graft while receiving none of the kudos, let alone pesetas. When they finally dry out or get clean and their senses kick back in, they will realize just what the owners are up to and they will want no part of it. They will quit the game. Sure this takes longer for some, me I suppose by way of example, but eventually it will happen to everyone on the ranges. The bosses don't fret over this, however, as they view it as acceptable collateral damage, the inevitable fall out from attrition.

I've had enough of it, Billy told me one night after we had just returned from the pub.

Enough of what? I asked him, for Billy was the kind of guy who had had enough of many things. To be fair, he had endured a hard time, but strangely with the advent of a new Duce his star was on the ascent.

This fooking crap life, he told me miserably. He had told me this many times and I had always been able to inflate his sagging morale with comforting words of wisdom; even then I was an old head on a young, rather girlish, body.

Nah, don't be stupid, I cajoled him, you're just having one of your turns that's all, tomorrow you'll be fine, just like you always are.

I miss me home, he continued, me dog, me pigeons and me mates, there's nowt down here for me.

It'd be foolish to give it up now, Billy kid, I told him, trying to sound like one of his own. I had picked up some of his accent and in such times of crisis, of which there were many, I attempted to communicate with Billy on his own level.

Me dad's found me a job near home, a big hotel – I can finish me stuff there, see?

And me?

You're different from me, you're one of these people, I'm not, and never will be.

I'm no more one of these people than you are Billy, that's just depression fucking with your head – 'ave you been takin' those tablets Rex gave you?

Those tablets were worming tablets for dogs!

And?

That's what I mean see, you just cruise through, the brigade leaves you be and the girls go all gooey over yer, but not me – I want to chat up me own kind.

Ain't those chambermaids your kind? They're from way up north kid.

I hate fuckin' Geordies, I want good rosy-cheeked Midland lasses, see!

And ferrets?

Aye, and me ferrets, me pub, me darts, me pigeons, me ...

Flat cap and clogs, by gum? That got him laughing at least – maybe Rex had something a tad stronger, I'd ask him tomorrow ...

The thought of losing my own personal Tonto got me edgy. We had travelled a hard road together and stood shoulder-to-shoulder through many traumatic events, and now suddenly it really looked as if I would finally be going it alone. All I could hope was that Billy awoke in the morning and decided to forge on; after all, he'd done it many times before.

But he didn't. Instead he woke up with a steely resolve and penned a resignation letter in shaky handwriting, and that morning he handed it to the Duce and returned to the kitchen somewhat relieved. The deal had been done and there were no hard feelings, there never are in hospitality. In two weeks' time Billy would be leaving for good and when that day arrived I knew that I would feel as if I had suffered some kind of amputation – reaching out for an appendage that was no longer there. Right about then I fucking hated everything about hospitality and my mood became dark and unctuous, like old fat.

Our salad days were over, and all that remained was to salute them. And celebrate we did, chefs being the best people in the world to have around you when you are young and at a miserable loose end. The joie de spirit that prevails and the quantities of alcohol that materialize out of thin air are always sufficient to perk up even the most desolate of situations. We partied high on the hog with other people's money, sometimes with no money at all, and each and every service during those two weeks took on an air of joviality as the brigade as a whole, at least what remained of it, got together like a gang of skinheads looking for a fracas to gatecrash.

On Billy's final night the drinks flowed into the kitchen like a river of bitter and afterwards everyone went disco crazy to see Billy off in style – what with our friends from college and other assorted hangers on, by three in the morning the dance floor was awash with paralytic chefs doing the Freak. I had been given a rare weekend off by the Duce and the following day I accompanied Billy to the train station where we would part one last time, he to his ferrets and me to my folks for a weekend of catching up. We stood on the platform like breaking-up sweethearts, neither too keen to have the final word.

Well, this is it then, Billy said in his pragmatic northern way.

I guess so, I replied.

We had a few laffs, huh?

Didn't we fucking just. You take care now Billy lad, give that new kitchen hell okay?

You fooking better believe it.

We shook hands and Billy boarded the train. As it shunted out he dropped his pants and gave me one last big white moon. We said we'd catch up, but of course we never did.

After Billy left, the veneer of professional cookery cracked for me, in fact, nothing's been quite the same since.

Back at work on Monday the Duce called me in to his office. They do that when you suffer a terminal loss. He gave me the pep talk and told me that shit was changing. I could see as much, the Duce had a large metaphorical broom and had developed a broad sweeping action with it. The two older apprentices had already been offloaded. The Duce was adopting a youth policy, something that has become all the rage. The tall gangly kid K had decided to switch his allegiance to a career in waiting and swapped to the general catering program. Only Chu remained, and surprisingly he and I became rather good friends. The tramp and her twin, those two incestuously conceived sisters who had made my life a living hell for three months, had scuttled back north, hauling their own embryonic version of Rosemary's baby. The Duce told me I would be moving on up, he had me on the fast track. Two new fools were coming in at the bottom and one was to be a girl; the whole mood of the place was shifting precariously toward modernization and in many ways that was good. But in many others it wasn't.

That afternoon I was called by management and informed I was to move rooms that very afternoon as my and Billy's old room was to be prepared for the arrival of a dozen waiters from Luxemburg. I was still on the way up, however, by about two floors.

After two and a bit years of cohabitation, you kind of become used to those midnight chats about dodgy curries, Danish girls who turned out to be boys, the state of the union, the shithouse, intestinal tracts. To have your own digs is considered a luxury. It means privacy, silence, undisturbed sleep, no perverts dressed in female underwear trying to kidnap someone outside your room – all of which is fine and dandy, but it takes some getting used to. I had been in institutions of one sort or another all of my life, first at home, because what is the family if it is not an institution, then at Her Majesty's pleasure and then straight into a life of slavery. And all of that time I had grown accustomed to the two-up bunk-house routine.

But not any more. Now I was on cellblock D, a dead-end corridor with a bathroom at one end and five rooms in total. It was me and eleven chambermaids – whoever thinks up these strange accommodation billets? What was considered an all-girl corridor now had a new inmate, and to be sure they did things wackily up in cellblock D. For a start, they had a small TV room – small being the operative word, but, it saved traipsing down to the second floor to the communal lounge. They had lines strung the entire length of the hallway where their smalls and other personal attire hung, now that we were Bumble-free, and the bathroom was like a cross between a beauty salon and a Chinese laundry. The landing reeked of incense, cheap perfume, hairspray, drying laundry and cigarettes. Bumble would have been in his element in such an environment. It was a dramatic change from what I had been used to, but as you know, I am a chameleon and I can adapt to any given set of parameters with consummate ease. Thus, within a relatively short space of time I was considered to be one of the girls – and as recompense for such a heartfelt welcoming to the other side, so to speak, I made it my business to make sure that my girls got fed better. This is the way it works in the big hotel; where once we were resentful enemies, now we were quite happy scrunched up on the sofa watching TV while squeezing each other's zits. I told you I was no misogynist huh?

I think it all stemmed from that pimple cream, the skin-toned cream one of the girls lent me. The kitchen is full of grease, globules of the stuff floating around in the humidity looking for pores to invade. Blackheads every fucking where – pop, pop, pop, we were all at it.

Anyhow, she gave me this cream. It was fucking bronze, and I said to her, Jesus, I look like I've got fucking foundation on!

Don't be a bairn, she scolded me, it's not quite your colour but it defines your lovely cheekbones, I wish I had cheekbones like those . . .

Never mind that, I told her, I can't go down into the kitchen looking like this!

Why the hell not, pet, you've got the lashes and the nails, foundation is the obvious step.

This'll never wash, not as pimple cream, those sons of bitches will chew me up and spit me into the pig bin.

If I didn't like the cock, pet, if I was into the old belly-slapping meself like, then I'd be all over you like honey, pet.

And what does that mean?

Nothing, she shrugged.

And you think I ought to turn up for work looking like this do you? And with these bloody ringlets too! Four curlers you said! Look at this lot!

Wear your hat, no one'll notice.

Fucking Jesus Christ.

So, as you can see, all was going well. I had been indulged up on cellblock D by a gang of girls happy to indoctrinate me into the ways of the woman. I had endured leg waxing, eyebrow-plucking, hair dying and even goddamned curlers in the name of assimilation – I had become a bona fide aficionado of the pain game. Understandably, the Duce and my comrades somewhat frowned upon the idea, especially when I first arrived for work with nail polish on, but it was the seventies, glam was still big and the world was changing. A new era of androgyny was being ushered in, and no one was too bothered, even though some still recalled how messy the whole Bumble incident had been. Then the Duce requested my company once again in his mansion, where I had my own stool.

Luiz, he said, kind of fondly, but then his demeanour altered. What the fucking hell is that crap on your face? What the hell's up with you?

Pimple cream, I told him, and luckily the foundation hid my blushing.

How would you like to go to Paris? he said, quickly changing the subject.

What, today? I answered, caught off guard.

Not today you little fuck, a week on Friday, we're trying out an exchange program.

Sure, I said, not quite convinced of the merits of such a plan.

Great! the Duce said, which gave me another queasy feeling – maybe I wouldn't be coming back?

Don't worry, the Duce said reading my mind. It's only for three months.

Why me? I asked, as I made to leave after a polite curtsy.

The Duce looked at me very oddly, a sort of distasteful glance, and then he studied my rather well-shaped eyebrows and neatly rounded fingernails. Well, you just look the kind who'd enjoy it. I had no idea to what he was referring. Paris, huh? That was a swinging joint – okay, the girls would miss me for sure, but if I knew them, they'd soon find some other fool to manipulate.

I was off again, this time across the Channel like so many good Englishmen before me. Little did I know that fate had begun to roll out a welcome mat for me that would once again see me mired in the company of women. It was a pattern that was taking a foothold and once entrenched would never budge. Isn't it queer the way fate pans out?

30.

A Glass Of Champagne

I looked absolutely fabulous. I had this deep-red velvet jacket, a Rolling Stones T-shirt underneath (the one with the big lips), the widest pair of Brutus jeans and a pair of white platforms with four-inch heels. My hair was all golden and ringlets, very long by this stage, and it's no wonder I had to fend off innumerable pick up ploys – a lot of them, I might add, from nouveau Euro men.

I was going to Paris, something bizarre would happen there, some kind of revelation, I just knew it . . .

It was a bumpy trip, it always is, and before we had even upped anchor I was pining for the white cliffs – I felt it to be my duty. In Calais they were building what looked like some kind of prison for asylum seekers or British boozeheads on the rampage for duty free; the place was bleak and desolate and I was glad to be on the express train though I had not the faintest idea of where it was heading. Having only been on French soil for forty minutes I understood only too well that these people couldn't even comprehend their own language, let alone anyone else's.

The French train system, however, is not at all like British Rail. The French have developed a people-moving system that actually serves the desired purpose of conveying people from

A to B without the necessity for detours and three-hour changeovers. Their engine drivers fair whistle through towns at a speed that makes you clutch the armrests for safety. If the speed doesn't kill you, then passive smoking will – but no one is unduly alarmed, the French have their own way of life and they do not give two fucks for either the health or mental well-being of anyone else.

The nearer I got to Paris the more agitated I became – this has always been my way, I speak first and consider what I've agreed to later, which is not always the wisest principle to live by. At the Gare St Lazare I disembarked clutching a small map that the English had given me – and of course it was as useless as a screw-in light bulb for a bayonet fixture. What to do? I knew I was close to the large black cross on this stupid motherfucker of a map, but close in such circumstances is nowhere near enough to ensure safety. I backtracked into the teeming station and waited patiently in a queue of disgruntled French types to get to a ticket window. The man behind the counter was wedged into his seat as if he had once been trim but had grown into an accepted appendage. He was chewing a cigar – I mean where do you see that kind of action these days? I slid the address of the hotel I was to reach across the smeary counter top and he looked at it as if it were contaminated by rabies. The man was of no use whatsoever, not to the railway, France or himself. Fortunately a young lady behind me stepped in to assist. She led me outside and gave me a rudimentary walking route.

You must look for the maison close, yes, the bordel? Le quartier des prostituées, oui?

Hello, I thought, what kind of mess have you walked into here Luiz, you gibbering fool? The lady was nothing if not persistent. I thought of yelling out for a gendarme, there were two across the street in capes smoking cigarettes while idly frisking a deadbeat. Now, however, the lady had taken hold of my arm; I thought she intended to hump me someplace, and me having only fifty francs. Finally, obviously having had a gutful of my Anglo-stupidity, she pointed to a sign barely visible down the street, and shoved me in the right direction and went off muttering words that sounded blasphemous.

Phew, that was a close call, I muttered, just keep going up this street and if you can't find the place after a mile call it quits and head back to the station. You might still catch the night train.

I did find the place though, much to my initial regret. It was a tawdry joint that had seen better days, perhaps around 1912. Hesitantly, I ventured into the dank and eerie reception, where the light was about the strength of two candles. I handed my letter of introduction to the man behind the desk who studied it surreptitiously. The French have a rather annoying habit of taking an eternity to read anything, as dinnertime would later prove. Apparently they can drive around like speed freaks on acid but when it comes to reading a letter or a menu it must be perused in great detail, as if it were a directive from the Pope. Behind me a geriatric woman sat on a faded chaise longue tapping a walking stick on the linoleum. Finally, after a decade, the man behind the desk grunted, then struck up an animated conversation with the old madam – and then they both fell silent and studied me intensely as if I were meat on the hook.

The woman leapt up with the speed of a cat about to be neutered and took my arm with her gnarly claw. Just as I went to strike her, the clerk interceded in stilted English. Yes, I should go with the crazy old woman – to bed, oui? What? In the sack with this old hag? Not fucking likely, not even for a million francs and scrambled eggs for breakfast. Yes, yes, go, the man insisted, while the crone summoned the strength to drag me toward the door – she was surprisingly fucking spry for a hundred-and-forty-year-old.

As we walked, she kept rabbiting on at me in French, saying things like 'de jeune fille' and 'une jeune Anglaise', and then pinching my arse as if I were a veal calf. Finally we reached another building outside of which were about twenty girls who had also seen better days – in France they have a phrase that means 'mutton dressed as lamb' but in England we call them 'hookers'. Are you fucking sure? I accosted the old lady as she started to push me up the steps.

Oui, oui, she insisted, de petite amie. When in Rome, huh? So I gave up struggling and let the old bitch lead me to a dark room. Whatever would be would be, I guessed, and I was just too shagged to fight. The whole sorry mob of them would probably gang-bang me and then chop me up and toss me down the sewers – and I hadn't even collected my holiday pay yet. Hadn't the Duce and F&B told me that this wasn't a holiday, that it was a pilgrimage?

Just like the hotel, the street, the area, this maison had seen more favourable times, most likely under Nazi occupation. The old woman, let us call her Madam P, kept coming into the room – to check that I hadn't escaped, I presume – then insisted on opening and drawing the rickety old blind numerous times, obviously convinced I had never seen one before. Ah, de jeurne fille, she sighed contentedly as she pinched my cheek. It was never like this in Eastbourne.

The madam was still living in the twenties. Absolutely certain that Pound, Hemingway or F. Scott might pop in at any moment for tea, she fussed around all over the place ushering girls here and there, and every time I closed my door, thinking I was finally alone, she would open it again and rebuke me.

Jesus H. Christ. So I lay there while various women of the Parisian night went about their business, stopping intermittently to wave at me or smile. Maybe they thought I wanted one 'on the house' just to be going on with?

Those stupid bastards back in England had sent me to a fucking whorehouse as some kind of jolly prank – I bet they were laughing their butts off right now, either that or they really didn't have a fucking clue, which would go a long way to explaining why it took so long to win the fucking war. It turned out to be a hellish night. The brothel did its briskest business of course during the dark hours, and certainly both it and the part of Paris I found myself ensconced in, cared little for sleep. The street outside was abuzz with activity: fights, drunks, pimps, hookers, taxi drivers, foreign tourists haggling over prices, gangsters, and most likely chefs too. At some ungodly hour, and I cannot tell you which one for my watch had already been filched (most likely by the old hag) a writhing living sculpture of nakedness fell into my room. There was a bolt on the door, but, of course, no damned catch, and the three of them – gender unknown – rolled around the place like eels. I was too tired to complain and after some short while the fracas fell back out onto the landing where the hag appeared and began beating them all with her cane. It was déjà vu after the Billy incident.

The French do not apologize for such incursions – in fact, they never apologize for anything. I had read somewhere that the worst thing the English ever did was liberate France, and now I understood why.

I had a fitful sleep, dozing with one eye open, one hand on my wallet and the other on my nuts – you can never be too prepared. As dawn broke I listened to the early morning Paris serenade: delivery trucks, trains, crazy people just roosted from their doorway slumber, hungover drunks and disgruntled foreign types yelling at shuttered windows. I had not eaten since Dover and my stomach was not at all happy over the matter, so reluctantly I tiptoed off to find food. Downstairs, Madam P was asleep in a rocking chair wedged by the front door. She had incredible hearing and, on floorboards that played like a badly tuned piano, I made it not one full step before she jolted awake as if just struck by lightning. Thinking I might have to wrestle her to gain my freedom, I looked around for some type of weapon; after all, she was armed with a cane herself and I am all for the fair fight. As she made a grab for me I stepped backwards and hit my head on the coat rack. Her bony old liver-spotted hand shot out like a barb and caught a handful of my golden locks – I knew I shouldn't have let those crazy chambermaids put ringlets in it.

She did not pull me to the floor as I had first envisioned, instead she just played with my hair a while, smiling contentedly, then suddenly whacked me on the leg with the cane. You crazy fucking bitch, I said angrily, what kind of a fucking set-up is this? The madam merely cackled and grabbed my wrist. And where's my fucking watch, you tea leaf?

She led me down the passageway as I thought about strangling her, but my stomach rumbled loudly and she cackled again. I could smell coffee. In a small room a gaggle of Parisian working girls sat around a large table covered with pastries and coffee pots. The air hung heavy with cigarette smoke and the smell of oysters. After they cleared a space for me, I squeezed in between two of them and immediately grabbed for a croissant, making the girls and the madam laugh. While I gobbled they began examining me the way explorers used to examine apes. It was not the start I had expected, but I suppose it could have been worse, they could have put me in with the bums.

I had no idea what was happening, whether I was expected to make my own way to work or what, and besides this there was no clock in the whole damned place. One of the girls, a world-weary type called Marie, who looked as if she had spent the past night humping the whole back line of Les Bleus, spoke pretty good English. She explained to me I was rooming here as Paris hotels didn't have much space to spare; it was normal custom to board out staff to the lowest bidder. They would come for me at eleven, she supposed, that was the time they started work, did I know much of Paris? I told her I didn't know squat, and then I had to go through a long-winded explanation of what squat meant. I ate as I talked, it is not good table manners I know, but in Paris you must seize what opportunities come your way. As I reached for my tenth croissant the hag whipped out her stick and rapped me across the knuckles. Anglais cochon! she rebuked me sternly. The girls laughed and then we went through the pantomime routine as Marie translated questions from the other girls and my answers. Most of the questions concerned whether I was a boy or a girl; in France they are very open-minded about such matters; usually, however, they put the foreign boys in with the trainee Legionnaires.

After some time Marie asked me if I needed to wash, if so she would show me the bain. So up we went, up the creaky old stairs to the goddamned attic, a tiny room with a chipped old yellow hand basin, a shower cubicle with neither a screen nor taps, and a low-slung kind of dunny with an odd plughole. Marie came back with a threadbare handkerchief, large enough to pat your face moist on a warm day, then proceeded to enlighten me as to fundamental plumbing etiquette in the French capital.

The hose from here was attached here, like so, oui? Then

this knob was turned, but slowly, mind, lest I flood the whole damned place. And then this knob and that cock and the water would be lukewarm for about twelve seconds after which it would revert back to Seine water. Often, the hose got blocked, which meant there was merde in it. I was all for adventure, but even a person as easygoing as me draws the line at some stage. There was no lock on the door, the French do not believe in such things. Hesitantly I stripped naked and began fiddling with the goddamned knobs while holding the hose in my teeth like a filthy junkie.

No sooner had I some water than I leapt under and began to scrub at the grime Paris had already covered me in. The door flew open and a half-naked whore began running the cold tap in the basin just as casual as you fucking like. What trickle I had became like ice and I had no option but to step forward and grab my toast-sized towel to cover my shame. The woman gestured, did I want to use the basin too? Hell no, all I needed to do was find my way back to my hovel, only I hadn't a clue where it was. In the midst of this chaos another woman appeared, walked over to the funny-looking shitter, hoiked up her skirt and promptly sat herself upon the throne. Then Madam P – and god forbid that she strip buck-naked too, but no, instead she giggled and cackled to the girl squatting on the throne. Afterwards, I asked what the crazy old loon had been saying. The whore lit a cigarette, and told me as best she could in translation. She say, maybe it best you face truth, huh? And then she stared at my crotch, hard, the way a cow goes misty-eyed over a clump of grass. The French are very liberal, except when it comes to kinky sex, or so they told me later. It was always the English who had the most bizarre and disgusting tastes, which is something I have heard said a lot during my subsequent travels.

After an hour of going in the wrong doors I finally found my room, which looked as if it had just been ransacked. The bedding was gone, but the bugs still clung gamely to the mattress. I went downstairs and sat in the foyer; eventually, I supposed, the hotel would come and find me. If not, well, who really fucking cared?

A boy turned up around midday, or at least I guessed it was around noon from the shadows on the sidewalk. He asked me a question in French and I looked at him blankly. His name was Henri (On-ree) and he was here to escort me to my death. He thought it was funny, but I felt it to be an accurate summation of my dire situation. I walked up to that place like a man en route to the guillotine, stepping every so often over piles of crap on the sidewalk. The French are filthy people and I don't think they will mind me saying so. Parisians, perhaps, are filthier than their countrymen, but this is to be expected if you are going to urinate in gutters whenever the urge strikes. Eventually we reached the backdoor of the hotel via a long and complicated sewer route and Henri led me in to be slaughtered. Paris hotels have a weird kind of entry and exit system going on, they have entrances on many levels and on different streets and for the uninitiated the whole thing is a brand new kind of hell. I had no will for it; my legs were like rubber and my mouth as dry as a well-made martini, why on earth had I volunteered to come to this place when there were far more suitable candidates back on the ranges? It's the Romany blood in me, on my mother's side, they were all gypsies and proud of it – eternal wanderers – and when you have that kind of gene buried inside you, your feet and brain simply yearn for the open road. Ye gods, I needed somewhere to puke.

It's a shock to the English system, to be thrown head first into an alien environment where everyone loathes you and many deadly looking Gallic types stop whatever job they are doing to study you like they would a piece of ripening cheese. I have been in many such situations, however, and I know the ropes – the first French fucker who tried it on I would shaft with the nearest implement. The French have no stomach for hand-to-hand combat.

I am not the type to be intimidated, but I am the kind who will choose fleeing when it suits a purpose. Henri, who was quite a winsome fellow, took me over to a filth-strewn bench. How the French can produce the food they do from a place like this took me aback. Another chef, a pungent swine, brought over a bag of shallots and plonked them in front of me.

Oignons, he said indignantly.

I know what a fucking onion is, I replied angrily. The stinking swine smiled, then he strode off to have his back waxed in a nearby salon – and pity on the girl who had to strip the hair off a beast like that. Fucking onion peeling, these bastards just wanted to watch me cry.

An indeterminate time later, after many leering gooks had approached me and muttered obscenities in their native tongue, the brute re-appeared.

Mon Dieu! Dix! he exclaimed.

What, ten onions? But no, this bastard had it in for me – he was the king of the block, as they say behind bars, a lumbering Neanderthal way short on motor neurone skills. He started dumping bags of onions on the bench with a savage smirk on his lips, like a lion about to eat.

Ten fucking bags, are you insane? I yelled. My rantings drew the attention of the whole filthy crew and they were circling menacingly like rabid jackals in Pango Pango.

Usually when you have to bring down a beast such as this it is wise to be mob-handed. A slingshot won't do the trick, despite what fucking David said. Big animals such as these, however, have one weakness, and that is their size. They are wild swingers and if one of those blows should catch you then for the love of Christ you are gone for all money – but get a big fucker like that down and you have the advantage. This is a wise adage that the gypsies have always used to great effect. Now the brute was accosting me in universal sign language and the inference was clear; this big motherfucker had designs upon my orifices, maybe a trip to the charcutier where he could dry-hump me until sundown, who knew? Jesus H. Christ, would I always be condemned to a life were I had to slug my way out of insane situations I had leapt into?

Probably yes, there is no other way to survive.

In the end in makes little difference how these things unfold, so long as you do not capitulate and let the filthy bastard have his way with you over a sack of shallots. There is nothing to be gained from servility like that, apart from internal bleeding. Why me? I bet that that kid they had back in Blighty wasn't trying to stave off a gang of pastry geeks with well-greased hands. No, that fucker was probably sitting down to a full English being feted by the brigade and dribbled over by the girls, just like that drunken bastard Gyson. No wonder he had been keen to get three months out of this shit bog. I would have words with the Duce when I returned, if, that was, I ever did.

Goddamn the fucking French to hell – hadn't Wellington said the same? It was now or never, either I stood my ground or cried like a baby; this pig had his honour and his reputation within the brigade to maintain, though I could see he was hesitant – that was his biggest mistake, that and the fact that his puny brain had convinced him that I was just an English pansy with golden ringlets.

I thought briefly of Agincourt, but Henri stepped in and grabbed my arm like a queer vamp in an underground club and led me away from the scene and out to another part of the kitchen. Then a manager appeared, the way they always do – after the event has taken place. He grilled Henri about what had occurred and I got the impression Henri was in fact defending me.

I wondered what Billy was doing at that moment, and how come it was me faced with the most intimidating of situations, yet again. But I did not have time to dwell too long on such points, it was service time, and when that time comes, all petty bickering is put aside.

They do things differently in Paris. For example, they appear to prefer being in the shit bog and this way they can keep prep to the bare minimum. The kitchen is not regimented as it is in England. There is a brigade, but it is not run on draconian authoritarian lines as it is elsewhere. All share equally in the work, and this way they deal with food as an experience rather than a product. It is not unusual to find the saucier in the pastry section whipping up sabayons or parfaits, nor to find the garde-manger trying out a new adaptation of forcemeat on the ranges.

They drift seemingly without care, but always with the eye on cross-pollination, and this is why they understand the principles of food, and how it should be used, far better than the English. One minute you can be helping on petit-fours and the next plucking wild birds; you might find yourself skinning fish and the very next moment working on soufflé mixes with a pâtissier. When you prep it is always immediately before service and almost everything works in the a la minute mode; the French are not fans of blanched vegetables or big pots of demi that can still be used three months later, tasteless or not. Usually they will make stocks, but only small quantities, not the large vats we made in England, and they are hot on flavour and texture, on feel and touch, on smell and first instinct; if something is not quite right they will discard it and never worry that the patron or waiter is waiting. Let them wait, is their mantra, we will cook at our pace and produce what we consider acceptable – never compromise on quality for other more trifling concerns. That is a sound philosophy and we would do well to heed it. The English tend to work at fast pace, frenetically, and if you study an English service you would be struck by how manic it can become – the raised voices, the speed, the blur. But not in France.

There, it really is like theatre, and they have no aversion to intermissions between acts. It is not casualness, but professionalism. As a rule the French do not overbook their restaurants with gluttonous swine and as such there is a harmony between the restaurant and kitchen that you never find in England. You do not, for example, turn up for work to find that the crazy maître d' has booked in fifteen tables of geriatrics from the funny farm just for the money. In France they will turn you away like a pig-dog if they are happy with the amount of covers they have booked. It is all very civilized, as much of the French way of life is, and where I had first assumed they preferred the shit bog, after some time I was able to understand that they didn't even know what such a thing was.

And during all of that calmness they are keen to talk with you about sex. Making love to an English woman is like humping a side of pork, they told me. I took their word for it, having never had the opportunity to make my own comparison – pork in England is too expensive to indulge in that kind of caper. The English are too reserved on some matters and too bizarre on others – this is why the Common Market was no good. The French take their sex seriously and, as a result, have no time for things such as monkey business.

Wot iz it, zis monkee bizness?

Hum, you know, it's when people fool about just for the fun of it.

Ze fun of it?

Yeah, hanky panky, gigi gigi oui?

Merde, anky panky?

Ye fucking gods, it doesn't matter anyhow because it ain't my cup of tea.

Wot? Ze Engleesh, always wiz the cup of tee! Yuk.

I was at the forefront of the formation of Franglais. When universal sign language failed, we would converse like this, in half English and half French, and the trouble with three months of that is that you find it an incredibly hard habit to break, much like constipation and the urge to cross-dress.

Back at the brothel we had all settled into a workable routine and even the madam had desisted from attacking me with her damned cane, and that was lucky for her. One by one I began to learn the girls' names and gradually I was able to converse with them. The prostitute's life is not a merry one, although it is better than being a poultry worker – at least I think that's what Jeanette said. Still, we all have our crosses to bear, and mine was no heavier than anyone else's. In France you do not get two consecutive days a week off, at least I didn't – and perhaps this might have been due to the management impression that a kid like me could get into serious trouble in a place like Paris. I settled for Thursday and Sunday and in a way that split saw me through the experience. I had no time to become bored or homesick although every time I went to leave the building on my day off the hag would call for one of the girls to escort me. This became known as the happy hookers' tour of Paris, a great name for a series of guide books, for who knows a place better than the resident whore? The trouble with it, however, is that I never actually knew where we were at any given minute. It is nice to have a hooker on your arm in the sunshine, but not when she is happy to drink away your pay like water. And those girls know how to drink, let me tell you.

First we went to the Parc du Champs de Mars and along to the Eiffel Tower. It is just a pile of rust, Cissy told me, and no one likes it apart from foreigners. She was not the kind of girl prone to gilding the lily but she knew every rat-infested bar within a rat's leap of wherever we were. The days off passed this way – to the Champs-Élysées with Alice, the Place de Breteuil and the sewers with Jeanette, the Place de la Concorde with Marie, to the Left Bank with Gertrude, and to the Quartier latin with Jacqueline. And then it would start all over again and after a while we all began to enjoy it – for some of them it was the first time they had seen a Paris institution other than the Bastille, which of course most of them had probably been in, so it was kind of nice to see it through my own eyes and theirs too. The prostitutes really are the soul of the city, I suppose, any city. They understand it and they keep rhythm with it. Despite their initial teasing and cheek pinching and jolly pranks, these whores really were a grand group of girls. Well, not girls, women. When you wake at four in the morning and find a whore asleep aside of you, it is then you realize how comfortable they are with you – and that you can take heart from the fact they considered half of your bed more comfortable than a whole chaise longue.

It is oft said that the French, and Parisians in particular, are a hedonistic bunch; I have no quarrel with the argument because to me they are. It is life they enjoy – the simple things: good bread, a glass of wine, a walk in spring, friends, conversation, the joy of the spirit. Apart from sex, they do not take matters too seriously, and perhaps all of this stems from the fact that they were an occupied nation and upon liberation they celebrated their freedom and have continued to do so.

The English are forever worrying about things they cannot change – they spend their life scrimping, saving and planning with one eye always on the past and the other on a future that rarely comes. The French live the other way around, in the now, the past is past and the future will take care of itself. Every day is quite possibly the last, and in a city with maniac freakhead drivers such as Paris it is a very sound philosophy to live by.

On my last weekend in Paris I was rather downbeat. The girls were off to their annual ball, the prostitute ball, I guess, where hookers from our area let their hair down for a night, so to speak. I do not know who first broached the crazy notion that I should go too, but once it had been said the whole lot of them thought it an absolutely fabulous idea. I on the other hand wasn't so sure – the thought of being at a prostitute's ball was kind of exciting, but, somewhat frightening, too. I am all for the risqué, but not if the upshot is a night in the cells being manhandled by grubby drunks. They assured me, however, that it wasn't a night of debauched carryings on; it wasn't a work night, oui? When you are being harangued by a half-dozen French prostitutes hell-bent on getting you to the ball on time, there is little you can do apart from acquiesce.

After all, they had been very good to me and as such I owed them this much at least. That was how, four hours later, I came to be bundled into a taxi looking like a Paris whore. Now, you will appreciate by this stage of our journey that I am not one who is prone to making astute decisions, but, as they say in Paris, life is for the living.

They were having their gig at what looked like a disused church, which lent the proceedings and the fast-gathering assembly an air of blasphemy. Upon arrival small glasses of some obnoxious drink were thrust into my hand.

The night wore on at a fair cracking pace and the horrible drink helped me shed inhibition – not that I was ever what might be called inhibited, no indeed, my life is an open book. If, however, you have attempted to dance the stomp in a ridiculously tight skirt and dangerously high heels while tanked full of potent liquor, you will immediately understand what the night was like, and if you haven't, then I recommend it. My head was in a state of foggy funk and I recall only two tunes that seemed to play continuously, that 'Glass of Champagne' thing by Sailor, and more oddly, 'Waterloo' by Abba. I felt like I had been singing about Napoleon all night and by dawn we were out on the streets continuing the revelry. You can do many things in Paris, and one you might enjoy is to catch the metro in drag – it is all very French and in the spirit of the times. The drink turned out to be Pernod and I have never drunk it since, as I spent all of the next day hunched over the toilet vomiting foul yellow stuff that smelt like aniseed while the old hag berated me for hogging the only flushing toilet in the whole joint.

The following day I was at the Gare feeling flat and badly hungover; we drew many admiring looks from the station crowd, the hag, six prostitutes and me. It was cheek kissing all round, a few tears and good luck. They hoped I would be back and I assured them that I would. As I climbed wearily aboard the train the crazy bitch of a madam struck me one last time in the gooleys with her stick and laughed like a wild dog with a full belly.

I slept till the ferry. The crossing was particularly rough and although I am a good traveller it shook up my guts too much for me to enjoy it in any way. When I first saw those cliffs again my heart plummeted. I had no inclination to go home, and no willpower left to resist it. I was dog-tired and deflated, a person who had gone to Paris and willingly sold their soul to the she-devils. I had taken the boat train to perdition. And now I was coming back completely altered and with no gumption for the struggle ahead. The thought of work the following day made me sick.

I rode the train. It was a wet and windy night, and when I alighted, all the shops were boarded shut, two winos were fighting over a half-bottle of cheap port, a dog barked crazily at the moon, and all my ghosts kept mocking me. I was home again.

Only I wasn't, because this wasn't even my home. In fact, I suddenly realized, as the wind rocked me back, I didn't even have a home any more. Tom, the night porter, let me in, and it was like I'd just popped down to the newsagent for a paper, not returned from three months in Paris. I crept upstairs, not really wanting to see anyone – not wanting that still-fresh image of Paris interrupted by something or someone from this other life. I wanted to hold onto that memory for as long as was possible – which in a big hotel, is almost impossible.

In the dark of my room I lay still, making no sound, nothing that would give away the fact I was back. I didn't want to go to work tomorrow, not go down to that kitchen and pick up where I'd left off, because to be honest, I couldn't even remember where I'd left off.

And where was Billy when I needed him?

I should just quit, pack up and move on, my time here was over, it could never be the same again. In fact, I could never be the same again . . .

31.

You Make Me Feel Like A Natural ...

When you are away from your job for three months, your position changes. Hell, in a big kitchen three days is sufficient to see your perch dismantled or, indeed, given to some other feathered variety of suck arse.

In my enforced absentia the Duce had been on a free-signing purge and had recruited a platoon of slipshod gooks. No Duce wants a brigade full of little Bocuses running about the place knowing it all; what he needs are good reliable plodders with just enough mush to grasp the bare essentials but not enough grey matter to further investigate.

My hands are tied, he told me wearily not long after I was back in the mix. Times are hard and the boys upstairs want to see some results. Anyhow, how was gay Paree?

Fine, I told him, a step up from a slum like this. The Duce eyed me menacingly, he knew my style, had always recognized that I was a loose cannon.

That Frenchy Alfred was a real whiz anyhow, he continued, worked like a sheep dog.

Indeed, I thought, and right now he is probably back in Paris telling them what swine we are. That's good then, I replied.

I hate to tell you this, he began hesitantly. When the Duce

hates to tell you something you can be assured that actually he loves to tell you whatever it is.

What? I asked.

Well, we've got this new gun, Robbie, on the sauce, all the way from bonnie Scotland and he's doing so well that for now I'm rostering you into the pastry.

I shrugged, nonplussed. I had learned many lessons in Paris, just like Wellington.

Just until we reshuffle, okay?

Take your time, I said as I made to leave. I'm happy enough.

Not that I was, but it wasn't going to the pastry that depressed me. That was a cushy gig compared to busting your balls on the line. Besides, it was about time that my allegiances shifted, I had spent too long playing the game from only one perspective, and not only the game, life too.

At least in the pastry you get a lot of time to think, to brood on all of those little concerns that are niggling you. Pastry chefs are deep thinkers, more philosophical than the rest of the mob, which is why the mob despises them. Anyhow, I was going to enjoy it, the crème caramels, the éclairs, the tourte St-Honoré, the bavarois, the babas, the gâteaux and the brandy snaps. There is a lot to enjoy in the pastry. And I have always had a sweet tooth.

I do not understand why, but some people take offence over the smallest matters. This was one of the more unsettling aspects of cookery as a job. There is always some numb nut that feels put out, snubbed, incompetent, frustrated, and jealous over something quite ridiculous, like hat sizes.

These trivialities, left unattended, will fester like an open sore, and before you know it there is some gun-swinging goon staring you down over a stack of still-bleeding rump steaks.

It was beginning to drag me down. I had spent my entire life fighting one way or another: at school, at home, at football grounds, at chow time and slop out, and in kitchens, and my fervour for the fisticuffs was waning. I was too good-looking to risk serious disfigurement at the hands of a part-time pugilist with a phantom beef. But these reasons, sane as they were, were insufficient at that juncture of my life to curb my hotheadedness. I had always lived that way, an angry young man with too much lip and too much spirit. No one was going to come sit on my bed and tell me there was a better way, that chivalry was the better part of valour, that I could do exactly what I pleased and damn the consequences. Life isn't like that, kitchen's aren't like that, and yet ... that freak Bumble had done it, hadn't he? If a shithead like that could make the dash for personal freedom, then why not a kid like me? Shit, I was ten times better equipped than Bumble to swap sides, I had it all: the hips, the legs, the pout, all I had to do was find the courage to ...

The Duce yanked me out of the pastry after the veg chef went down with a heavy dose of scabies – it's the onions that give it to you. Still, I didn't really mind, the veg is not a hard section to handle and after a week of that I was suddenly told I had to do two weeks of breakfasts. That did unsettle me, I always had an aversion to that particular gig. However, when the Duce peals your bells you must stay in tune. At least on breakfast you could be relieved of the evening service, as you begin at some heathen hour like five in the morning and finish at lunch service after you have re-prepped the following morning's breakfast trays and made the potage de jour. On breakfast I would feed my girls, and to be sure it was the best feed they had had since the breast. And that was how my fresh set of problems began.

There grew from my acts of treachery the idle notion that

I was playing favourites. These same whingers had also taken offence over the fact I lived on an all-girl landing. When my feline cellmates got wind of this, they began defending me during their thrice-daily visits to the hot plates. The fat was well and truly in the fire and spitting nicely.

Passions spilled over during a lunchtime service when I became embroiled in a tinderbox situation regarding the state of the staff meal. The goon serving it was a new scar face and he was in the Gang. The girls were moaning that the stuff was putrid and inedible, and to be sure they were right, not even a starving dog would woof down such rubbish. I told the guy, politely, that I didn't think the shit could be eaten, and he told me to keep my fucking queer face out of it. On occasion, you can let remarks like that slide, but this was not one of those times. The goon was itching for a bout and I could see his neck veins bulging and his fists opening and closing; there was not a single bead of sweat on his heavy-set brow. Given the slightest provocation, an animal like this could do me serious harm and my reputation would be shot to fuck. The girls were watching too, which made it worse – either I stuck up for them or I took a hit, and that is the goddamned Devil's choice.

He let me have a good one right in the mouth, then another for seconds that squashed my nose, and then a third – he was a greedy son of a bitch. I did not go down, however, that is not my style. Instead, I allowed the blood to pool in my mouth and as he stood there all pulsating veins and rippling muscle I spat it straight into his face. That riled him even more and as he grabbed me by the jacket someone finally had the good sense and decency to step in. If they hadn't, that guy would have torn me limb from limb.

For the next few months I would run the gauntlet of abuse, and kitchen boys being kitchen boys, they clung to their own brand of intuition – gut feeling they call it – 'better that limp-dicked son of a bitch Luiz than me'. To them I was a bad seed, something neither here nor there, indefinable. I flew with the girls, and as such I must surely be a queer. Boys are quite stupid when it comes to such matters, and at the top of the stupid pyramid you will always find a rat-faced English boy.

It takes me a long time to admit I have had enough but, when I do, I can act swiftly and decisively. And that was how I came to throw in the remainder of my apprenticeship and walk away with my battered pride and a deflated ego, oh, and some good advice on make-up techniques. I had no qualms about quitting, I was sick of the whole filthy lot of them. Let them keep their schoolyard rules and their inane ways, no one needs to live like that, and especially not someone as gifted and good-looking as me.

So you're off? the Duce said matter of factly, as if I were just going on a long weekend.

I am, I replied, maybe hoping he might show an interest in talking me out of it, even in an insincere manner.

Well, I'm sure you'll do okay wherever you end up.

This is the Duce, the very same Duce you eased into his job, the very same Duce who used to be your second-in-command, letting you go because it suits the bigger picture.

I'm sure I will too, was all I remember saying. I went up to management and arranged my paperwork. It was all shuffled rather quickly, and, as I really didn't have anyone I knew at that joint anymore, not YG who'd long since quit to form a punk band, not Herman who had gone to Switzerland, not anyone, I just upped and left.

I did have one night of revelry with the girls, out at some

club, and I got some good advice, affirmation of advice I'd recently received in Paris. I felt better, as if some terrible burden had been lifted off me both mentally and physically. I went home for a while, back to the nest, back to the old man hogging the shitter and the old girl moaning about TV. That couldn't last – I wasn't any more a part of them than I was of that hotel I'd just left. But where to now?

32.

Go West

All I knew was that I had a star-crossed skill and for the sake of my own sanity I had to move on, and quickly. So I did, to the west of England where the sun never sets. That is horse-chestnut country, cowpat cunt-ry, and down there the only black beauties you're likely to see will be handed you in capsule form by some half-bred gook still wearing milking boots.

It was a small place, five in the kitchen and I was third in command, or indeed, third from the bottom if you look at it pessimistically, which some are prone to doing. I ought to have known there was something dicey about it, though at the start it all seemed pretty normal – as many others have said while they sit in five-by-five cells on death row.

It all became as clear as aspic however, not long into the trauma-riddled tenure. I had a guest room, digital clock, TV, one of those gizmos that makes tea – all the mod cons – a clear view of the girls' high school directly opposite and the work, was, yes, interesting. The owner of this fine establishment, let us call him Mr C, was as bent as a dough hook, and that is all well and good as I am no homophobe; a man can do as he pleases so long as he keeps his paws off of my sweet arse, that is a rule of mine and it has never been one I have felt inclined to bend. He was a knowledgeable man, anyhow, a true epicurean; he preferred his meat French.

I was enjoying the morning bread-making, the lively banter, and the Anglo-French repartee; we were a united happy team. And then they had a staff party in The House. I do not know who arranged it but that is of no importance. What is, is that sometime during this drug-fuelled hayseed revelry a local girl quite a way under what authorities call 'The Legal Age', started to scream hysterically about RAPE then locked herself in the second-floor bathroom and began projectile vomiting. Ye gods, it was not a scene I was happy to be around, not even on the fringes, because incidences like these have a nasty way of spiralling badly out of control. The second chef told me that someone had to shimmy up the drainpipe out front, see if the bathroom window was open, and somehow get in and unlock the door.

That makes sense, I told him, as I watched a French waiter run by me with an axe.

Well? he said.

Well fucking what?

You're the skinniest – I've got to stop that Frenchy from chopping the door in!

Me? I can't climb up drainpipes. What do you think I am, a common criminal?

This is no time for pedantics, he told me angrily. Someone has to get that crazy bitch out of there before the pigs arrive, the people on this street are law-abiding taxpayers and they don't much care for this kind of gig.

I saw his point, although it was no skin off my nose whichever way the mess panned out, I hadn't even seen the girl before. I am all for pitching in, so without further ado I went outside and scampered up the drainpipe like an intoxicated weasel. The window was ajar and as I clung to the pipe with one hand I started to reach through and pop the window catch with the other – until the girl started shrieking hysterically and tried to force the window shut on my bare knuckles. This girl was off her face on some jungle potion and we began a crazy struggle. She had the advantage because she was inside, although she was all but naked and standing precariously in the bath, skidding on her own gut stew. Finally, however, I yanked the window open. It flew outwards, almost knocking me from my perilous position. Why didn't those stupid fools just break the goddamned door down instead of standing behind it shouting abuse? Eventually I fought her off and she fell backwards on the floor. As she did I fell through the window and into the bath, and consequently into a pool of steaming vomit. It was a hot stinking mess, there was puke every damned where, like *The Exorcist*, and the girl was scrunched between the toilet bowl and the wall shivering uncontrollably. If I let the mob in now they'd tear her to pieces, and probably me too. It was ugly and I was right bang in the epicentre. There was no way out of it now, once you are in the mire that quick shit will suck you down faster than a dopehead does cough syrup. I had to slap her, it was for her own good. She was babbling incoherently and scratching at the walls like a bog hound. As I tried to ease her out of the nook, she lashed at me savagely and slit my lip with one of her bright red fingernails. The incriminating evidence was now so huge that not even a top-drawer lawyer would take it on.

Get up you crazy bitch! I told her, and stop this goddamned fighting, I'm here to help you for fuck's sake. She began to regain her senses and stopped shivering, while I kneeled there in the puke trying to establish just what had set this crazy scene in motion. She hadn't the faintest idea. She was out of it, a real fucking space cadet, gone for all money. I told her I was going to open the door and she grabbed at me wildly and begged me not to do it. Jesus H. Christ, I was doomed for certain this time, and then some fool on the other side of the door yelled, Don't do it Luiz! You letch!

That was all I fucking needed.

No one knew who the girl was or how she had gatecrashed our soiree. This shit just happens sometimes without rhyme or reason, but one fact was certain, no one in that house was a rapist – I had seen such beasts before and these boys were not of that ilk. What could we do with her? What should we do with her? Where did our moral obligations begin and end? And that was exactly what the jury would be pondering when this whole investigation got into the System. I didn't like it, not one bit. Someone suggested we pump her full of coffee and throw her over the fence at the bottom of the garden, let her wander the train line and all lock ourselves in our rooms and forget about the whole sordid debacle. I even found myself buying into such a wanton and debauched notion; sometimes it is better to just cut the problem loose and tank up on cheap wine or anti-freeze.

But not tonight. For one, the girl was attached to me like a leech and despite my best efforts I just couldn't shake her off.

She'll have to stay here, some jailhouse shrink ventured.

Stay here? I started. Where? But people were already scuttling away like roaches when the light was flipped on. Now she was my problem. What was it going to look like when the fuzz or her extended family, maybe both, busted in in the middle of the night wielding billy clubs and pitch forks and found a dishevelled teenager hanging limply on the arm of a wild-cat chef? Oh yes, I could see the headlines now, and my immediate future – through vertical bars.

Despite all of these legitimate concerns, I could not find it in my heart to let this bedraggled girl wander the streets. That was how I came to spend a frightful and desperate night on the downstairs couch with an underage girl hoping that by some miracle salvation would arrive, or that she wouldn't wake in the morning thinking it was me who had done the dirty on her. Each time I got up to leave she would grab at me like a giant squid; whatever had happened to this girl had scared the living crapola out of her.

And where the fuck were her legal guardians? Didn't they realize their teenage daughter wasn't in her own bed? I repeated a good male mantra: soon it will be dawn and my obligations will be spent.

She woke with the mother of all hangovers, but not in any vindictive or accusatory way. Her story was a shabby one, much like mine, although, I agreed, she had much to be ashamed of. In fact, her home was thirty-odd miles away and she had stumbled into our midst after a vicious argument with her boyfriend and, by all accounts, well, hers, he was a poxy-faced geek whose only credentials to pilot a girl like this about the night were a student union card and a learner's licence. She didn't know what she had taken, or drunk, only that she had been overcome by fear and paranoia. We've all been there, I told her, been overwhelmed by those monsters.

I walked her to the bus stop and waited, I was pleased to give her the money. Keep it, I told her, just never mention this night to anyone ever again, or you'll damn us both to hell.

I think I love you, she said.

Don't be fucking insane, I reprimanded her. Thankfully, I had already given her a false name and if she ever came calling again, it would be that knee-jerk of a French waiter who took the flak.

After that near miss we all settled down, again a happy crew, a little gang of good food disciples keen to etch our names into guidebooks the land over. Mr C was big on ratings and as a consequence we always had to be on our guard for inspectors. What a heinous fate the chef's is, forever at the fickle whims of pencil-pushers, dope fiends and wayward women. Mr C could smell a food inspector from across the hills, the way a bear is attuned to candy bars. Often, however, he was wrong, and we would disrupt a service that until that juncture had been going along nicely just to bend over backwards for some overweight creep who had no affiliation to good food guides whatsoever. One can never be too sure, Mr C preached, and to be sure his motto paid good dividends in the longer term.

But that was not the worst of it. Yes indeed, where there is one gay there will often be found another, and so it proved. Mr C's partner was a Canadian; let's call him Mr A to keep things simple. I don't know what it is about Canucks, but for some reason they have always unsettled me – and as you know, I am not easily unsettled. There is just something odd about them, many people have said the same.

It didn't take long. Mr A was a leery letch, a filthy, sticky-pawed pervert with no more interest in good food than a junkyard dog. He would fly over the pond business class for one week every month and treat the place like it was his own private bordello. Everyone was on edge and no one was safe unless they were female. Breakfast was the worst, you were alone and no sooner did you have the wholemeal flour ready for mixing in the Hobart than the dirty old sod would be in the kitchen with just his robe on. He derived some sick kind of pleasure out of discussing his breakfast requirements half-dressed, and his hands were like two over-active grouper fish. It was a bad gig and I didn't much care for it – although obviously he cared for me. I found myself constantly on breakfast when Mr A was in town, and everyone else was happy that the dirty bastard didn't like their scrambled eggs. This kind of action can wear a person down, and a person with a quick temper can be prone to rashness – and that is why I came to be in Mr C's office explaining how and why I had clubbed his lover to the floor with a K-beater from an industrial mixer.

Look boss, I told him, I'm all for parity and equal rights, okay? Fuck who you like, but, man, just keep your filthy lover's paws out of my pants, okay? That kind of sordid gig might well wash in Ottawa or someplace where everyone's schmoozing around like beavers on heat, but not down here in chicken-coop country.

After that, it was never quite the same, the two of them took a queer disliking to me and when that happens they will look for any excuse to cut you out of the herd.

It wasn't my fault that the deep fryer caught alight either. I was nowhere near the damned thing. One of the gimps was frying the innards out of whitebait fritters when a well-bosomed waitress with rosy cheeks drew his attention momentarily away from the thermostat. Women are like that; they swear that they loathe people ogling their goods, and then attire themselves to make ogling almost unavoidable. Still, that is not a part of this story. I saw the blue haze first when I glimpsed up from my station where I was filling tiny little vol-au-vents with crab and fennel. That doesn't look right, I recall thinking, since when has the air been deep blue? And then WHOOSH! FIRE IN THE FUCKING HOLE! There was pandemonium as people fled and the flames began savagely consuming the ceiling in and around the inadequate extractor fan. Those stranded didn't move. Their pupils were heavily dilated and their mouths agape. I glimpsed the waiter out the corner of one eye, he was moving toward the inferno with a jug of celery in his hand. NO! I yelled – had that crazy Frog thrown that jug of iced water and celery into the inferno we would have ended up being sieved from the ashes the following day while loved ones, or those with some other vested interest, carried around dental charts.

Next thing we were all outside on the grass having a smoke while the ceiling was pulled down with crowbars. The night was warm, if I recall. It had all happened in a flash.

But not the recriminations – they dragged on like smouldering tyres. The fire had caused considerable damage and someone was responsible. I knew who it was, that shitface who should never have been allowed anywhere near an industrial fryer. But these errors of judgment occur periodically in professional kitchens.

It wasn't my fault that I fell on the flattop either. No one in their right mind would do such a thing just to accrue sympathy and brownie points – there are easier ways. It was all due to a quince. I had never seen one before and was oblivious to the fact that if I slipped on one in clogs I would go arse over tit. Why was a fucking quince on the floor, anyhow? That is sloppy procedure and someone was responsible – but not me.

I was doing my meez, getting ahead of the Game and keeping my head down. Bad vibes were buzzing around; rumours whispered that I'd slept with an underage child – ye gods, the way some people twist things to their own bizarre gossip tastes. Of course there was still the fact that one of the owners of the joint was in hiding until the K-beater brand left his face, and then there was the Great Fire. Just keep your head down, I told myself, and all of this will blow over like a dust storm in Kabul. And it would have, too, only I hadn't allowed for the curse of the quince – or was it a fig?

I don't remember much about the episode, not after all that fucking morphine. I was on my way to get something, that month's edition of *Cosmopolitan* maybe, and then me and the fruit on the floor met. I was falling, and when you fall you stick your hand out. Only there was nothing to grab onto apart from the flattop, which is hot and large and insatiable, and it gobbled up my hand like a foreign tourist gobbles up boy flesh in North Africa.

In the immediate aftermath I didn't even realize, I just got up and thought, phew, that was close – and then all hell began to tango on my hand. I looked at it as if it were detached, this huge giant balloon of skin where only moments before I had owned a reasonably functioning hand. And then the pain came – one big breaker of ball-busting agony that swept over me like volcanic lava. This is fucking bad, I recall thinking, you are an invalid, you will never masturbate again, god willing.

Someone came up, looked, went into hysterics. No one knew the procedure apart from the waiter with the jug of iced water and celery. He grabbed my arm, plopped my hand straight into the jug and the water hissed angrily. They started getting ice and clean tea towels and lawyers; this wasn't something they could make go away with burn cream. I needed a hospital and they scurried around playing rock, paper, scissors to see who would take me. Then the second chef turned up. He owned a big hog, a 750cc BSA or something, a black sleek beast that ate bitumen and spat flame. He crammed a helmet on my head, tied me to the pillion seat with an apron string, then burned rubber straight down the winding driveway. I held my arm out, the wind rippling my unwinding bandages as we rocketed through town with two panda cars in pursuit – they knew all about the goings on up on the hill, and here was a Hell's Angel with a chef on the back of his hog ripping up a quiet country town and trailing dirty linen to boot.

The Chinese locum doctor took one look at it, then smashed the glass in the emergency morphine cabinet as if he had been waiting for just such an opportunity. Within minutes I was floating on a tranquil sea of happy drugs, him too, as they began the saline-washing and gauze-wrapping business. That was too much action even for a hell-raiser like me, something had to give or I would be either dead or strapped to some piss-stained mattress staring wide-eyed at mustard-yellow walls while a nurse with hips a yard wide rode me to Bedlam and back. Good Christ, yes, I saw a light, and that light was red, white and blue and was held aloft by a beautiful stone-faced woman of liberty who said to me: Luiz, you are the poorest, most down-beaten weary son of a bitch I've ever seen. Why not quit that shithole and come play Russian roulette with me and the gals out in A-merica. Amen to that, sister, I remember whispering. Yes indeed, a boy like me could achieve big things in a country full of gun-wielding dopeheads with no sense of morality whatsoever, so why the fuck not? It all made perfect sense, in a morphine-induced kind of way.

Mr C didn't flutter so much as a false eyelash when I handed in my resignation. One of the waitresses went into labour when she heard the news, though. She had just recently ditched her French waiter boyfriend and had, apparently, set her sights on me. Well, hard shit, I had no intention of settling down in a farmhouse with the kind of girl who could breed like a rat. I was out of there. I'd utilized my time well, poring over those North American cookery mags Mr A hauled over as reference materials to disguise the hard porn. I wanted to go to America.

Oh, darling, why? my mother said, as I sat on the sofa at home reading my hate mail.

Why? Because I'm sick of this place, that's why!

Why don't you just find a nice girl and settle down?

To what?

Normal things.

As in?

Oh, I don't know, shopping, umm . . .

Yeah, well there you are, look at all these replies I've got to my letter of enquiry.

That's nice dear, will you be off soon?

Just as soon as . . .

Down on the farm I have found, everything reeks of horseshit.

BOILING POINT

Okay, you there, the ride's over, okay? Go home and get some sleep. Hell, but what a wild roller coaster it was, huh? I don't know about you, but personally I'm all but spent. My head hurts, my body feels like it belongs to some drug-dependent geriatric and everything is like one big giant red blur of madness. I need a break, and some heavy-hitting hormonal dosage, the way you feel at the end of shift – buggered. You give your all in the big white machine, it demands that at the very least, and if you can't or won't give that much, it will chew you up and spit you out.

It is 1980 when this piece of the story winds down, I have already given five years to the machine, and, in return, it has given me nothing. I am due to go to America, and I think I will, although what I don't know is that my paperwork will take another two years to complete and during that time I will have plunged into the bottom of many bottles. I will have drifted around the west of England like a gun for hire, and any chance of a glittering career would have already given me a wide berth. By the time I finally do get to America I will already be beyond salvation, much like my country of birth, which was already long past its use-by date. Still, that is another story, for now we can wipe down the benches, mop the floors and turn off the lights. In a few hours the breakfast chef will turn up, we hope. He will be straight from a bed he's probably never slept in before and the night porter will pump him full of strong coffee and pills hoping to coax him through another stint on the grills. The hotel will come back to life, the chefs will drift in, many unshaven and with very bad hangovers. Another day will start, another shit bog will form, many people will lose their heads, their jobs, their innocence. New people will turn up, old people will crawl away and die some place, and in the restaurant, as ever, the paying guests will be none the wiser to the dramas of life unfolding below.

No one will really give a hot flying fuck about food, that is all bullshit, fabricated for the ever-swelling ranks of good food publications. I never gave a fuck about food to be honest, I had more important things on my mind, and yet, strangely, I was a competent chef. With the right encouragement maybe I'd even have scored one of those TV gigs. After all, I was photogenic enough. But that was not to be my fate and maybe in hindsight it was for the best. Shit, everything that happens to you in life is for the best, there's no other way of looking at it, huh?

And so, we part, me to yet more therapy, you to whatever it is you do, whatever it is that gets you through the night. If you're game, I'll pick you up again, take you on another freakhead trip through the badlands. Look out for me; I'll be driving a big maroon Oldsmobile with enough room in the front for a dozen cheerleaders, a crate of something heavy and any hitchhiker stupid enough to climb aboard.

Then we'll cruise, just throw caution and good sense to the desert winds and suck up the great American dream ... roll right through that stinking bad-ass yellow goop where dreams, good men and dirt-cheap hookers all end up in a roach-ridden motel room while outside . . . the neon flickers mercilessly.

Until then, just bunker down. You know the drill by now.

GYSTG

Teri Louise Kelly . . . Adelaide, South Australia 2007
atta-girl@hotmail.com

Wakefield Press is an independent publishing and distribution company based in Adelaide, South Australia. We love good stories and publish beautiful books. To see our full range of titles, please visit our website at www.wakefieldpress.com.au.